BLACK

For The Love of Heroin

Stephen E. Crockett

Edited by Common Newman
Cover by Fred McAllen & DARLENE
Photography by Dusan Zidar

Second U.S. Edition
Copyright © 2010 / 2017

1

This book contains explicit, descriptive use

of illegal drugs. It is a documentary pertaining

to the use of narcotics and is not intended to be read

by anyone under the age of 18 years old.

Cover and Graphic Design by DARLENE

Second U.S. Edition
Copyright © 2010 / 2017

ISBN-13:978-1979270250
ISBN-10:1979270252

Printed in the U.S.

Here I lie in my hospital bed
Tell me, Sister Morphine,
when are you coming round again?
Oh, And I don't think I can wait that long
Can't you see that I'm not that strong

The scream of the ambulance
is sounding in my ears
Tell me, Sister Morphine,
how long have I been lying here?
What am I doing in this place?
Why does the doctor have no face?

I can't crawl across the floor
Can't you see, Sister Morphine
I'm trying to score

Well, it just goes to show,
things are not what they seem
Please, Sister Morphine,
turn my nightmares into dreams
Oh, can't you see I'm fading fast
And that this shot will be my last

Please, Cousin Cocaine,
lay your cool hand on my head
Come on Sister Morphine,
will you make up my bed
Because you know and I know
in the morning, I'll be dead
And you can sit around,
and you can watch
All the clean white sheets stained red

The Rolling Stones: Sticky Fingers: Sister Morphine
Lyrics © Abkco Music Company
Mick Jagger / Keith Richards Marianne Faithful3

Chapter 1

Starting anything is seldom easy. Getting this book off the ground has not been easy. Looking over my shoulder at the train wreck that is my past has been difficult to say the least. You should know, right off the bat, that at the time the events described in this book were occurring, I was working with very little information. If someone had told me there were things in this life I must resist at all cost I might have stood a fighting chance. My life would have probably turned out very differently. Unfortunately, this was not the case so when I look back I see a lot of dead friends, a lot of fractured lives, a lot of painful losses and a lot of time wasted on substances that do nothing to enrich the human experience.

Because of everything that has occurred over the past three decades I have retained little of my original self and I've had to fight the demons in my backyard on a regular basis and from an early age. Doing so takes a constitution most people just don't have and the fighting skills I needed to win such wars were always slow in coming. I must also admit I didn't always fight my demons as hard as I should have and I didn't always win when I could have. Something was always drawing me back into the darkness and as crazy as it may sound I have sincerely loved almost every drug that helped get me to the bottom.

For me, personal salvation did not come until I had wasted the majority of my life in love with things I now know are poisons. I ran with what little information I had and for me that was always changing. When looking back I see the demons of drugs and death chasing me down. For better or worse I have learned a lot from these wasted years. Unfortunately, these lessons were all skewed by heavy drug use and death. Life's lessons are not cheap. There are no discounts, no do overs, no free passes. The sooner you learn this the better off you'll be.

In my case, pain was the catalyst that propelled me. It was the reason I learned what I know and I guess you could say my response to pain and loss established the vicious cycle recorded in these pages. As I watch the people around me cope with pain I realize that the way you choose to deal with it makes all the difference in the world. Some people brush it aside and keep going. They act like it doesn't bother them. Like their hides are thick enough to protect them, until one day, one small thing, sends them over the edge and everybody wonders why.

Some hide their pain within themselves, where it rots and festers until it makes its presence known as a life threatening disease with the potential to kill them. Others hide from it or avoid it completely by self medicating with drugs or alcohol while others have the ability to study from a third party perspective in an heroic effort to learn from their mistakes.

Chapter 2

I do believe that with age comes wisdom, but not everyone who finds themselves tangled up in drugs has the opportunity to learn from their mistakes and move on. However this is an important step and you must learn to take it if you are to have any hope of freeing yourself and recovering. It's not only smart it's essential. Healthy minds focus on healing and forgiving, or adopting a more productive way to live. Painful experiences are rationally processed. Bad memories are slowly forgotten. Toxic people are banned and a new life is built with the express purposes of avoiding harmful situations. If you're paying attention you learn from your mistakes and this is essential to not just living, but to thriving.

You can't just keep making the same mistake over and over. If you do it will kill you in the end. For a precious few, loss and regret are factors that lock them into destructive mindsets. This type of person focuses on their injuries. Instead of healing and putting the situation behind them, they become fixated on the pain. They wreck their lives and fail to heal. They don't learn from it and move on and this is a painful way to spend your life.

I am very hesitant to apply the word "deserve" to the events that have shaped my world. "Deserve" is a very rare word, and that's a good thing. It can be used in both a positive and a negative manner. Most often it implies an action such as a "reward" or a "result." Very few words can cut both ways with the skill and precision as these do. Each define a good or bad outcome depending on how they are used.

For example; the reason you deserve something could be a result or a reward. It could be a result but not a reward. Or it could be a reward that is not the result you deserve. You may get both and deserve neither or deserve both and get neither. Deserve embodies the concept of "unintended consequences." In some cases "result" suggest the element of work while "reward" suggest a gift or positive outcome. Either way "deserve" is very tricky and there seems to be no rhythm nor reason to its application.

Chapter 3

Or is there?

Let's put the idea of "deserve" on the back burner for a moment and think about the concept of karma. Karma is simply a way of looking at life as a system of rewards and results. Karma is a very simple way to understand the word "deserve." Simply put, karma means that what goes around comes around. Do unto others as you'd have done to you. For very action, good or bad, there is an equal or opposing reaction. So if you do good deeds, karma will bring good things to you, whereas if you do bad deeds, karma will fill your world with bad things. Karma can be viewed much as a bank. Good deeds result in karma credits while bad deeds result in karma debits. The objective is simple. Live a good life, help everyone you can, be honest, treat neighbors as family and you will be blessed with good karma.

On the other hand, bad deeds result in karma debt. A single bad deed is a karma debit. Karma debits are like bad credit. You have to work them off like you're paying off a debt, which means that for a period of time you have to do good and incur karma credits that don't go into your karma account but are used to reduce your karmic debt. You must continue to pay off karmic debt until it has been zeroed out and then you can once again enjoy the benefits of good karma. Good karma keeps us healthy, wealthy and wise because you learn how to be a good spiritual person as opposed to being an unenlightened person. Your karma bank account fills with good credits leaving you with zero karma debits.

However, when a bad deed has been committed it is important to make amends as soon as possible so that you don't incur karmic debt. Those who guard their karma in this manner understand the idea of instant karma. The universe will not allow you to walk around with a lot of karmic debt. You pay off karmic debt instantly. If your karma debt is severe it may take years, perhaps even a lifetime to pay it off. The universe is exact and karma will rain down like fire on anyone who thinks they can carry a heavy karmic debt.

Karmic debt produces miserable lives. Going to prison is one way of working off a severe karmic debt. An indebted life, meager existence or menial job from which you cannot escape are all ways to work off karmic debt and none of these are productive ways to live your life. Karmic debt causes you to miss out on the good things in life and makes it hard to grow spiritually, mentally and emotionally.

When your karma is clean and your credits are high, the world is a wonderful place to be. The universe grants you options and you spend your karma credits wisely. Your interest turns into your employment, your job introduces you to good people and takes you places you may have never before imagined. All because you are properly managing your life. Good karma is also protection. Like a trusty shield good karma helps defend you from bad karma.

Viewing your life through the prism of karma teaches you to avoid bad karma situations. You enjoy life, health and wealth, and all that comes to you, does so with your spiritual temperance in mind. Everything is balanced in a way that fulfills you and makes sense. You become a spiritual beacon. The right people are drawn to you and you help them. You are drawn to the right people and they help you. This is a wonderful way to spread good will, which in turn produces more karma credits for you.

However, these rules are not written in stone. Karma is just a theory and bad things happen to good people everyday. Sometimes events seem random. The universe does not appear to favor some over others. In fact, bad people often enjoy the rewards meant for good people while good people often seem saddled with the luck of a person with serious karmic debt.

Maybe people create their own good or bad luck. Maybe things are so random that life will never make any sense and you just have to take what comes your way. Or maybe, with a clear head and a keen eye you can navigate your way through the pitfalls and landmines of life and through careful planning and judicious management enjoy life. Two things are certain: you will never make it out of here alive and if you expect to go through life with your eyes closed and get handed the best it has to offer you will be sorely disappointed.

Chapter 4

Karma is a constant reminder of the importance of keeping your life clean and your relationships pure. If I had understood the transitive consequence of the word "deserve" or the mechanics of karma at an early age I am quite sure that my life would have went in a different direction. Karmic principles are observed by many the world over, and I do believe that if I had understood them in my youth as good as I under-stand them now, my life would have turned out very differently.

The truth is I've made my share of mistakes and been party to things that have spiraled out of control. Along the way people have died and while not directly responsible for their deaths, I was there. As a result, I've have had to deal with the loss of friends while battling the daily grind of drug addiction. It has been said that what doesn't kill you makes you stronger. But what if it's like the word "deserve?"

What if the thing that's supposed to be making you stronger is actually trying to kill you? What if it keeps coming at you, relentlessly, day after day, night after night, year after year, until it has worn you down to nothing and you simply fade away?

What if its plan is to drive you insane and what if it all started with a dream?

Chapter 5

If taken at face value you may think this point of origin to be ridiculous and if you've never lived it you may find it hard to understand. But a lot of people have been inspired by their dreams, or followed their dreams, avoided bad situations or reaped incredible rewards because of their dreams. It has also been said by a wise poet that if you; "lose your dreams, you will lose your mind." This suggests that your dreams are very important to mental health and if carefully observed they can be very enlightening. As a result they can protect you with their insight and there is useful information to be gleaned from them.

History is replete with kings and rulers who viewed their dreams as portals to the future. They had wise men and scholars ready to interpret any dream that might come their way. The Bible legend of Joseph and the Pharaoh's dream is a well known example of the relationship between a dreamer and his seer. Dreams are still viewed as warnings, sometimes of good things and sometimes of bad. Not everybody puts a lot of stock in dream interpretation, however before you think it impossible for a dream to chart the course of one's life, let me explain how a single dream influenced my entire life.

To do so I must return to the last two weeks in the month of August in the year 1972. At the time I was twelve years old at the time and for almost ten days, during the miserable, irrepressibly hot, dog days of summer, was in bed, fighting a rare case of phenomena that brought with it a high, stubborn fever. At my most sickest, my fever reached 104 degrees and held its ground for a good forty-eight hours. If not for cold baths and compresses the fever could have easily cooked my brain resulting in my death.

During this period of extended fever I experienced an hallucination in which I was neither fully awake nor fully asleep. In this distressed state of mind, my mind endured a psychotic break that caused me to experience two distinctly different sensations at the exact same time.

On one hand, my nightmare began when the walls of my bedroom started rippling like waves of heat radiating off mid Summer asphalt. On the other hand, I was whisked to the top of a very tall snow covered hill. Dealing with two incredibly different mental states at the same time was like having my brain torn apart. Doctors would later described this mental disturbance as a fever induced "night-terror" however, the idea that it could properly be described as schizophrenia has also been tossed about.

For a twelve year old child who knew nothing of what was happening to him this dueling nightmare was terrifying. If it had only been a one time occurrence I would have connected it with my sickness; compartmentalized it and moved on. However, the scariest part about this hallucination is the fact that it has plagued me all my life. Forty years after that first night I am still dealing with this dream. At night it is a dream of terror while by day it is an hallucination.

In my original, fever induced hallucination I found myself standing barefoot and in my pajamas, on the top of a very tall, snow covered hill. In the distance I watched as the walls of my bedroom burst into flames that quickly engulfed the room. I look down at my feet and notice I was standing on the edge of an icy path that ran down a steep incline into unknown darkness. I could not imagine what lay in that darkness but a great sense of danger emanated from its cavernous depths. Fear twisted my guts into a knot while anxiety washed over me and I felt that I should run away as fast as I could.

However my room was now totally engulfed in flames so returning there seemed impossible and before my addled brain could formulate a different plan, an invisible force pushed me violently from behind, knocking me off my feet and sending me careening down the hill on my stomach. My speed steadily increased as the path grows narrower and narrower. Suddenly the wind battering my face turned into a choir of garbled voices which came at me from every direction, swirling around my head and trailing off behind me. They echoed from all sides as if I was sailing down the inside of a bowl. At a certain point these invisible voices turned into an insane laughter that swirled around me and sliced through my brain like shards of broken glass.

When I finally reached the bottom of the bowl the laughter faded away and the voices returned, filling my brain with their haunting, long forgotten chant. Fire flashed above me and the smell of smoke filled my senses as the swirling voices whirled around me like a tornado. Were the voices inside my brain trying to get out, or outside my head trying to get in? I didn't know. I couldn't tell. Either way I had no control over them and they didn't go away.

When I reached the bottom of the bowl, I leveled out for a few seconds and then started up the other side. When I reach the top I sailed out into the pitch black darkness of space. For a few seconds I flew straight up, free and clear, higher and higher, away from the crazy voices and the insane laughter left singing in the bottom of the bowl. When my forward momentum will carry me no further, I stalled and for a few seconds I just hang there, suspended in the darkness. Then with a simple "pop" I disappeared. I turned from my human self into a puff of smoke and powder that was quickly lost in the icy darkness. I was gone, simple as that. There was nothing left of me and I never came back.

Chapter 6

After several intense days I recovered from my fever and returned to the life of a twelve year old boy. However I began experiencing the hallucination that had accompanied my fever while I was awake. It would only last a few minutes and it can best be described as a series of sensations.

First I could feel it coming upon me, like a tornado, grinding its way toward me from a way far of. It would get closer and closer until it entered my body, twisting my guts and shaking my interior until it felt like my organs are being rearranged. It then went up into my throat, stopping my breathe and then finally into my brain where it played itself out as a ferocious panic attack. Overwhelming anxiety for a period of about fifteen minutes or so before it slowly backs off, just like it came, leaving me shaken to the core and that much worse for wear.

To make matters worse, the dream I had experienced during my fever became a nightmare that lurked in my sleep and became a source of great stress and anxiety. I dreaded going to sleep. I put off going to bed as long as my parents would allow and many nights I fought to stay awake just so I wouldn't have that dream. When I could no longer put off sleep, my brain would be filled with nonsensical voices and swirling insane laughter.

Eventually self inflected insomnia gave way to excruciating headaches and I had to sleep to alleviate the pain. Needless to say I was in a mental bind for which I had no solution. But, if I could make it dark enough I could sleep during the day. So I nailed blankets over my windows and tried to sleep every chance I got. However this behavior was hard to do or explain during my teenage years and while I told my parents what was happening to me, nothing was ever done to help me. So I ended up stuck between two worlds, neither of them good for my mental health.

Every time I had that hallucination something inside my brain changed. Every time I experienced that "pop" I heard it between my ears, in the center of my head, and every time I lost a little bit more of myself. A lot of times the nightmare ending "pop" would be followed by a "high frequency attention signal" that started as a high pitched whistle in my ears and increased in volume until it reverberated throughout my brain at frequencies and volume levels high enough to induce migraine headaches.

I have spent my entire life trying to defend myself from this hallucination turned nightmare, from my explosion into nothingness. its subsequent high pitch frequency and from migraine headaches that feel like aneurysms. Since their introduction into my life my only goal was to replace these terrors with dream free sleep. Unfortunately for me, trying to self medicate this mental health crisis ultimately led me down paths any normal person, with good karmic sense, would have avoided.

Looking back over the years there are two things that amaze me. The first is how that hallucination – in all its terror and insanity – revealed the path my life would take. Second is the fact that I'm still alive. Based on my personal history I know I shouldn't be. But for some miraculous reason I am. The reason I shouldn't be is because I have spent the better part of my life addicted to heroin.

This is not a subject I am eager to discuss. But it is a misadventure worth recording if for the sake of saving one life and therefore it is a story I want everyone to listen to. For me, the road that led from innocent young man to drug addicted adult began in 1976 when, during my sophomore year in high school, I smoked my first joint and drank my first beer. I was hooked on both straight out of the gate.

A prime contributor to my attitude toward illegal drugs was rock music. Many artist used their music to cryptically tout the use of certain drugs and once I had deciphered these musical tomes I was eager to experiment with them. This is no understatement and I mean it to be understood without equivocation. Rock music glorified the use of illegal drugs and lured me into my experimentation.

They made it sound like doing them was as natural as brushing your teeth. Ultimately the simplest of drugs, such as marijuana and alcohol, led me to sample every illegal substance I could get my hands on and this ultimately led me to the top of the illegal drug food chain. This did not happen overnight but as promised by The Grateful Dead, it turned out to be a "long, strange trip."

However, rock-n-roll music is its own cautionary tale. Musicians such as Janis Joplin, Jim Morrison, Jimmy Hendrix, Keith Moon, John Bonham, Tommy Bolin, Jerry Garcia, John Entwistle and Bon Scott died from heroin overdoses, cocaine induced heart attacks, pulmonary aspiration or alcohol poisoning. The plane crash that decimated the rock band Lynyrd Skynyrd was an unfortunate example of the rock- n-roll lifestyle as well as the untimely deaths of Jim Croce, Sid Barrett, Rory Orbison, Elvis Presley.

For its detractors, who described rock-n-roll as the devil's music, these deaths were a sort of perverse victory, or an affirmation of their anti rock-n-roll message and they were quick to say, "I told you so." The connection between rock-n-roll and illegal drugs was not lost on these well meaning prophets of doom. In their mind the two went hand in hand. Where you found one, you always find the other.

This is a fair description of the path my life would take. But getting from A to Z is not as simple as it might sound. My sixteenth birthday is an important milestone in this story because by then The Rolling Stones had put out three drug laced albums, *"Beggar's Banquet"* (1968), *"Let It Bleed"* (1969) and of course their tour de force; *"Sticky Fingers"* (1971). While the

Rolling Stones sang about drug use and the misery of *"Coming Down Again"* another British rock band by the name of Pink Floyd released a number of minor recordings that paved the way for two musical masterpieces, that while not directly singing the praises of drugs provided atmospheric soundtracks perfectly suited to enhance drug related experiences. These were *"The Dark Side of the Moon"* (1973) and *"Wish You Were Here"* (1975).

I was eight years old when I started listening to rock and roll music through a transistor radio my Mom had bought me for my eighth birthday. The Beatles was big, but relatively harmless, however it was the '60's so there was a lot of rock music to listen to and not surprisingly most of it dealt with drugs. From 1968 to 1978 the air waves were blessed with what we now describe as "classic rock." Back then it was music for children to grow up on and every year from the age of nine until I turned eighteen I heard my fair share of drug related rock music.

The Rolling Stones led the way, there can be no disputing that. Led Zeppelin brought up the rear and Pink Floyd gave the drugs a visual tapestry upon which to play and so between the ages of eleven and fifteen years old I listened these sound tracks without ever touching illegal drugs. Rock and Roll and illegal drugs went hand in hand. My 1978 high school graduation coincided with Pink Floyd's release of *"The Wall"* – a psychedelic masterpiece that has yet to be rivaled.

It is fair to say that despite the vast array of music produced during this period I listened to Pink Floyd more than any other band. I spent so much time in the altered universe their music provided that my friends started calling me "Floyd." When considering Pink Floyd's music it is also fair to say that I've been living on *The Dark Side of the Moon* the majority of my life. It is also worth noting that in the three decades which separate *"The Wall"* from the writing of this book, only one soundtrack has been released that even comes close to matching it in scope, depth and musical talent. That would be the Sixx A.M., masterpiece *"Heroin Diaries."* (2007)

Chapter 7

You may view this introduction as nothing more than random facts taken from a single, unknown life and that would be one way to look at it. However, they are the threads from which my first thirty years were woven and understanding them is critical to the story you are about to read. When looking back it appears I was destined to face the demons of addiction and death at an early age.

I say this because I've spent more than half of my life in love with a drug I should have resisted and I experienced the hook of addiction long before I understood it. I never learned to protect myself from the downside of drugs and there were aspects of my chosen poison that I truly loved.

I took my first Summer job when I was thirteen years old picking up eggs in one of Yadkin Counties many industrial chicken houses. But I didn't like working in that kind of environment so during my fourteenth and fifteenth year I delivered the newspaper to those who received it in my neighborhood. I turned sixteen in 1976 and took a job at a local grocery store, working part time on week days and all day on Saturday.

This was also the year I got my drivers license and I was able to buy my first car as a result of this job. When pinning my addiction to a specific date I always return to this year. So let's just blame it on the car and get it over with. Yadkin County was a rural farming community nestled in the foothills of North Carolina. The counties main employers at that time were tobacco farming or one textile mill.

Moonshine was rumored to be a cash crop although it was hard to pin the truth on that reality. If there were moonshine stills in Yadkin County it was because Yadkin was a dry county. Being "dry" meant that no alcohol could be legally bought, sold, possessed or consumed inside the county. This may well explain the high number of stills local gossip suggested were hidden in parts of the county.

It is also important to know that the legal age to buy beer at the time was eighteen and there was a beer joint at every county line willing to sell beer to anybody. If you could drive and had a car, you could buy beer. No I.D.'s were ever checked and that boiled down to a case of good old fashion competition.

I suppose, looking back, the general feeling at the time was that drinking, and getting away with it, was just a part of growing up. There were coolers full of beer and ice in every four wheel drive, at every cook out and on every fishing trip. In the summer we would float down the Yadkin River on over sized inter-tubes and beer was always a part of those outings. The local sheriff and police department handed out the occasional DWI, however they were never viewed as that big a deal. Make no mistake. Getting caught was a bitch. However, the right lawyer and the right amount of money would get a "Driving While Impaired" charge reduced to a minor traffic violation.

At this point in my life I would not describe myself as anything more than a casual user of alcohol and marijuana. In 1977 I turned seventeen and took a job at the textile mill Universal Fiber working second shift. I worked there during my last two years of high school. I never missed a day of school or a night of work. During this period I met Danny and Joanne. There were a few guys selling marijuana at work and after I graduated from high school Danny and I started smoking pot every day.

We worked second shift and never failed to go to work stoned. We were "stoners" or "pot-heads" if you like and we justified our daily habit by saying; "if we're stoned all the time, everyone will think we're straight even though your high. They'll think this because every time they see us, we'll be high and that will be their only point of reference."

We were teenagers indulging in our first illegal drug experience and I can personally attest to the fact that we enjoyed every minute of it. We should have looked in the mirror because the idea that a straight person couldn't tell if we were high was foolish to say the least. This nugget of drug based wisdom was dreadfully close to the cartoonish; "If I can't see you, you can't see me."

Chapter 8

After two years at Universal Fiber, management began to notice that there was an illegal drug market operating on their soil and they hired a local sheriff's deputy under the guise that he no longer worked for the sheriff's department. I didn't believe it for a second and I didn't like this type of scrutiny. If they knew this much it was only a matter of time before we all got busted. This thinly veiled disguise sent Danny and I running for our lives.

We both turned in our two week notice and spent the next eighteen months in our environment, jockeying for convenience in the bedroom towns and satellite cities that surrounded Winston Salem. My path took me from Universal Fiber to Chatham Manufacturing while Danny took a second shift job at Douglas Battery. We both moved from Yadkin County to an apartment in Kernersville. This was perfect for his job at Douglas Battery and I landed a job with Reynolds at their processing plant in Davie County.

It was there that my friend to drug equation blossomed like never before. I was nineteen years old and my weekly paycheck was incredible. Plenty of overtime was available and I was all to happy to work the hours offered. As a result my take home pay for one week was more than most people made in a month. The icing on this cake was the fact that the place was literally crawling with illegal drugs.

It was a drug abusers paradise, plain and simple. I was ready to sample everything available and it did not take long to figure out who had what. Everyone seemed to have something to sell. Cocaine, Valium, Marijuana, Quaalude's and Moonshine were just five of the many options found in the parking lot. It was perfect. I always bought large amounts of Valium to help me sleep and marijuana was everywhere.

I associated myself with the pot smokers because it seemed to be the drug of choice among the vast majority of my co-workers. At this point I guess you could say that my drug use was recreational. I drank beer on my days off, smoked marijuana daily and used Valium nightly to sleep. This combination guaranteed sleep and without them I didn't sleep at all.

However, it is fair to say that at this point I was most definitely in control of my life. I bought my own clothes, maintained my own car and of course I bought my own drugs. I had two things on my mind, money and drugs, and my world was flush with both. As a result I stayed high from lunch to dawn and it was not hard to achieve this goal. Saying that I had a one track mind would be an understatement.

Chapter 9

In addition to the regular menu of illegal drugs, psyche-delic mushrooms and LSD occasionally made their rounds. These drugs were never as available as my usual choices and while I experimented with these mind warping substances a time or two, they were the one sub-set of illegal drugs that I didn't much care for. I preferred to relax – to unwind, if lucky to sleep and to do so without dreaming. As a result, psychedelic mushrooms and LSD were not on the list of drugs I enjoyed.

I craved something I had yet to discover. Nothing satis-fied me. Every temptation left me wanting more and during my earliest experimentations I can honestly say I was disappointed. I should have accepted this disappointment as a sign from God and stopped then and there. If I had, I would have saved myself a lot of grief. However, at the time, my biggest fear was that there wasn't anything else out there to try. I never considered the fact that there was a drug waiting for me that could stop me dead in my tracks.

The Rolling Stones sang about "cousin cocaine" and that was a lead I pursued. Cocaine was a drug of mythical propor-tion. It had a style of use that interested me. Dump a little of that white powder onto a mirror, use a razor blade to chop and slice it into three inch lines, then snort the lines through the ever popular rolled up one-hundred dollar bill. The burn was in-stantly forgotten by the instant head rush.

A 3.5 gram "eight-ball" would last three days and I'd stay up for four days. But this was taking me in the wrong direction. I didn't want to be stimulated to the point of exhaustion and forced to stay up for days. I wasn't an uppers kind of guy. I wanted to relax, to unwind, to enjoy a mellow buzz that would end with me drifting off to sleep. So after a couple of encounters with cocaine I marked it off my list.

Chapter 10

Meanwhile, the crowd that introduced me to cocaine had something more to offer. Soon I was trying a totally new drug known as "MDA." MDA was a white powder that was sold by the gram and could be mixed with a little water and drank. It was not an upper or a downer but rather a mild hallucinogenic and a general all around feel-good drug. It was cheaper than cocaine, easy to ingest, and manufactured by a rogue scientist in the Raleigh-Durham area. MDA was truly a North Carolina invention.

As its use spread throughout the community it became known as the "love drug." This was because it made those taking it feel so good that making love was often an unintended result. A lot of interesting relationships began with MDA and the availability of a willing member of the opposite sex.

Today the molecular structure of MDA has been reconfigured and is manufactured in the form of a pill known as MD MA. On the street this pill is known as Ecstasy. But, in 1979 it was just MDA. Looking back I can safely say that my earliest encounters with MDA were a bit surreal. It definitely trumped any drug that I had tried up to that point. It was certainly easier on you than cocaine or LSD. Because of its availability and mellow attributes it quickly became my drug of choice.

MDA wasn't addictive in the traditional sense of the word. It was addictive in the sense that it made anyone who did it, want to do more. Another positive factor to MDA was that you couldn't overdose on it. Mixing it with water would let you do up to a gram at a time and there were never any withdrawal symptoms, just the nostalgic desire to do it again.

When it came to MDA, there was, as usual, a specific group of people involved. Randy, his girlfriend Donna, and Ricky were its original suppliers. They were connected to the rogue scientist who made it so knowing them and partying with them guaranteed unlimited supply and cheap prices. At this point in time I was just a simple user of MDA and I spent a lot of time with a close knit group of friends whose common denominator was MDA.

We were a good bakers dozen and a few of us are still alive. But the rest are not and I won't name names out of respect for the dead. I'll give the rest of them their fifteen minutes of fame, or infamy – depending on how you look at it.

This core group of friends would spend weekends together in various apartments, with curtains drawn and lights on low, consuming massive quantities of MDA. We would snuggle like lovers in beds or on couches, watching T.V. and making out. More often than not we would then nod off to sleep and wake up a couple of hours later ready to eat, shower and do more MDA.

We lived in an eerie MDA laced darkness and many a long weekend was spent in this strange universe. I most admit that I hated to see Monday morning come around because I knew I had to go to work. By the same token I was always glad when Friday afternoon rolled around for the simple fact that I knew I had a three day weekend, which I would spend doing MDA.

It may seem hard to believe but at this point most of us actually had real jobs and that is where our real money came from. We were more consumers than sellers of drugs and since our core group was quite large we needed a number of meeting places to accommodate our activities. So we had to rent a number of apartments. Of course that resulted a number of alliances and these could be quite fluid.

Drugs were our primary expense but there was also food, rent and electric bills as well as phone bills and cars that had to be maintained. Danny and I liked our apartment in Kernersville, however it was twenty-five away miles from Davie County and that was fifty miles a day round trip. So I moved to Clemmons, which was only five miles from Reynolds. I went in with Ricky on an apartment that was being vacated by our mutual friend Keith. It had been lived in by a succession of drug dealers and junkies and was known as "Hastings Hill Road."

There was no change in the lease. The rent got paid by whoever was spending the most time in the apartment at the time the rent was due. By the time of Keith's occupation, the apartment was generally considered a flop house. Its doors were never locked and the drug addicts who knew about it came and went as they saw fit. Every time I went to that apartment to hook up with Keith I saw people sleeping where they passed out. The reason they looked like they were sleeping was not immediately apparent to me simply because I didn't know what a junkie looked like.

Chapter 11

That makes Keith an important person in my story. I watched Keith shoot heroin on several occasions and I saw the buzz he enjoyed. I was intensely interested in what he was doing. I wanted to try it and Keith agreed to not only sell me heroin but to show me how to use it. So I studied how he did it and I took mental notes. Starting with the amount of heroin he put in his spoon, to the water that followed, to the way he used the back end of his syringes push rod to stir the powder and water together into a rich, golden soup.

Thinking back I remember how that spoon full of liquefied heroin looked like a golden eye looking at me, daring me to take the plunge. There would be no turning back. He cooked the heroin until it boiled and then he carefully pulled a small piece of cotton from an unused cigarette, rolled it into a tight little ball and dropped it in the spoon. He rested the sharp end of his syringe on the cotton ball, which he said was for filtration.

He then drew the liquefied heroin into the syringe. He then reversed the syringe so that its point was straight up, lightly thumped the air bubbles out. Once satisfied with his work, he cleaned the sharp end of the syringe in a some vodka that was handy, and had me hold down a vein in my left arm. A virgin vein that had no idea of what was coming its way popped up, ready to be abused.

And WOW, oh my god. It's almost impossible to describe the difference between what I expected and what I got. The rush was so incredible that it was almost sickening and the buzz that followed was like nothing I had ever known. It was love at first hit. Keith turned me into a junkie with one shot. The deal was that Ricky and I were moving into the apartment while

Keith was moving out. During this period Keith hooked me up with his heroin dealer and told me to keep my new-found skill a secret.

He was working out the details with his girlfriend for an apartment they wanted to share. Keith was an active junkie, however his girlfriend wanted him out of the drug scene. So he was trying to kick the habit while I was new to the habit. It didn't just happen over night but one day Keith was there and the next day he wasn't. With Keith gone the apartment belonged to me and Ricky.

Keith didn't take his furniture. Come to think of it, there wasn't much furniture to take. I didn't realize this at the time but his girlfriend had gave him an ultimatum, her or heroin. In the end he cleaned up his life and chose her. Looking back I can honestly say that she did him a huge favor. The only reason Ricky and I wanted the apartment was to have a place to party. This move sat me down right in the middle of the local drug scene.

There was no way of knowing this at the time but in a few short months Ricky and I would be the heart and soul of this local scene. Our apartment maintained its open house policy from day one and it was during one of these days that Ricky caught me shooting up. He immediately wanted to try it, so I gave him some heroin, showed him how to prepare it and helped him get off. I turned Ricky into a junkie.

Friends came and went, alcohol was always present as was MDA, Quaalude's, marijuana and of course heroin. We could get loud at times, particularly at night, but our neighbors didn't seem to care. To show them some love we threw back-yard cookouts and invited the entire building to come eat. And they all did – good food is hard to pass up. Those cookouts helped us become a community which meant our standing on Hasting Hills Road was recognized and accepted.

Chapter 12

This brings me to an important point. The illusion of sobriety was an important charade to maintain for a number of reasons. You couldn't drive around high on drugs for fear you would eventually have a car wreck or a run in with law enforcement and you can't go to work stoned if you wanted to keep your job. In addition we didn't rock out past 9 PM because we didn't want our neighbors calling the cops.

In my circle of friends, MDA was everyone's drug of choice and we all started out drinking it. However shooting it promised an even greater high. Within weeks of our first shot, Ricky and I were both active junkies and we introduced shooting drugs to those friends in our circle who was interested in trying it. My shooting drugs info came from Keith and Ricky shooting drugs info came from me.

I schooled a few of our regulars in the art of intravenous drug use and Ricky did the same. Here again we made it pretty easy. All you needed was a U-100 insulin syringe, or "rig" as we called them, a large spoon, a little fire, a little water and a piece of cotton for filtering, preferably from an unused cigarette filter. Dissolve your MDA in the spoon using water and a little heat, drop the piece of cotton into the spoon to filter, draw into your rig half full, invert the syringe and push out any air bubbles.

Then find an easy vein, slid the needle in, pull the plunger back just to make sure you're in a vein and once you see blood flow into the rig, push its contents into your body. The resulting high was addictive. No one could have imagined the intense rush shooting MDA – as opposed to drinking it – could be.

If you wanted to take shooting drugs to the next level there was a technique common among drug users known as "milking blood." Once your drug of choice was ready and you had tapped a vein, you pulled back on the plunger until blood flowed into your rig. This was the signal that your rig was actually in a vein. Then you pushed the blood and a small amount of dope into your arm. Pull back slightly, allow blood to once again enter your syringe and then push another small amount of dope into your arm.

This slow, steady process was repeated until all the dope in your rig was in your body and it could take an hour or more to milk one shot until it was gone. It was a safer way to shoot than a single steady dump because it reduced the possibility of an overdose. Milking blood regulated the flow of a large amount of drugs into small increments separated by intervals of time and blood. This made for a smooth journey of high after high after high all the way up to the most overwhelming high of them all.

It was also a good way to get the most out of a single shot. Junkies would sometimes milk a single shot for hours at a time. It was hard on your veins and in a way it was a waste of time but junkies did it. Neil Young knew exactly what he was talking about when he sang: "Milk blood to keep from running out."

Not everyone in our little group could shoot their own drugs and needed help from more experienced members. Those of us who mastered the art of self injection enjoyed the longest highs simply because we could reload our syringes at will and get off anytime we wanted to. We were only limited by the amount of drugs we had.

Chapter 13

There was no denying the fact that just a little pin-prick opened the door to a world of incredible highs. Shooting heroin was like having liquid Sunshine flowing through my veins. It was like being cradled in soft, warm, white noise. Nothing could reach you, nothing else mattered. It was simply the greatest sensation I had ever known.

After plowing mindlessly through every drug out there, I had found the one that would be the love of my young, junkie life. And it solved a problem I had been dealing with since age twelve. It gave me something I desperately needed; sleep. Sleep without dreaming. At first it seemed like a blessing.

No other drug compares to heroin. It permeates popular culture the world over and in many nations possession thereof will result in a penalty of life in prison while trafficking heroin will usually get you a death sentence. References to it can be found in popular music and literature and its list of famous users and abusers, real and fictional, are well known.

It is the drug of choice among actors and artist, writers and musicians for the simple face that it gets you out of the box. It brings things to your mind that you would never get otherwise. In his 1953 novel entitled *"Junkie"* William Burroughs draws from his own addiction to heroin to describe it as; "the ultimate merchandise. No sales talk necessary. The client will crawl through a sewer and beg to buy it."

In popular fiction, the character Sherlock Holmes is portrayed as an intellectual user of both cocaine and opium. According to its writer, Sherlock's only objection to using opium was that he did not like going to opium dens to purchase it. In one episode the author writes that his sidekick

Dr. Watson had man-aged to wean him from both. However, the episode ends with Dr. Watson stating that Holmes' addiction to opium was "not dead, but merely sleeping."

The Rolling Stones sang of *"Sister Morphine"* and *"Cousin cocaine"* while complaining about spending all their time *"Coming Down Again."* They promised that "their ragged company" would have their pain taken "away with a needle and a spoon." David Bowie released his cryptic *"Space Oddity"* as an autobiographical description of his heroin use and in a later song declared that *"Major Tom"* – the character in Space Oddity – "was a junkie." Guns N' Roses coined the phrase "Mr. Brown Stone" to describe their heroin use, while Sixx A.M., referred to heroin as the *"Girl with Golden Eyes."*

I don't think my circle of junkie friends realized that the music we were listening to was pointing us all toward our own death and that the Rolling Stones were simply leading the way. We were daring, crazy high, all the time, and living in time to the music. Looking back I think the most interesting thing about my first encounters with heroin was that the experience had a sound track created by junkies who were in no more control of their lives than we were of ours. It was an amazing duality and the only time in my life I have every known such universal comradely.

I was shooting heroin while listening to music that had been created by musicians who were shooting heroin, singing songs about heroin. Who was the devil and why did he need sympathy? Was Jesus just a shot away? Why would we need shelter and was a storm really threatening our lives? Would we really fade away? Should I take her in my veins and trust her with my life?

It's safe to say that over the centuries thousands have lost their lives to this highly addictive substance. Its list of famous victims is too long to recall. Its list of infamous victims is of course a lot longer. And then there was me. Once I tried heroin I lost interest in all other drugs. It quickly became my soul mate, the love of my young life. The epitome of perfection.

It filled me up, answered all my cravings and quickly became the only drug I cared anything about. I was only nineteen years old and despite my age, it felt like I had found the substance I would spend the rest of my life enjoying. Short sighted does not even begin to describe this point of view.

Chapter 14

You've heard of "mad skills." Well, shooting heroin is an "insane skill." I should note that even though this part of my story took place well before the discovery of AIDS and HIV, we were all very conscious of cleanliness. Liver diseases such as Hepatitis C and Jaundice were dangerous possibilities. We never shared needles and were careful to keep our syringes in tip-top shape by keeping them clean.

If you knew how you could resharpen the sharp end of a rig with an emery board, or the strike plate on a book of matches. A little Vaseline would keep a plunger siding in the cylinder so there were ways to get another shot or two out of every rig you had. But eventually an over used rig would no longer work which meant they had to be discarded and new ones pressed into service.

Heroin changed my little group of friends forever. Nobody seemed concerned about our use of MDA, but heroin was a different story. Some members of our little group were dramatically opposed to the introduction of heroin because of its negative connotations. Not so for me and Ricky.

Its effects were immediate and profound. Heroin hooks you with your first shot and from that point until it kills you, it becomes your daily obsession. I stopped using every other drug in favor of heroin and for the first time in my life I didn't have a job. I didn't get fired, I didn't quit, I just stopped going in and was simply replaced. I turned to selling MDA to support my heroin addiction.

My first heroin overdose was an accident. I pulled twice as much into my rig as I meant to and fired the entire load at once instead of slowly milking it. I don't remember a thing. I've been told I pulled the rig out of my arm, gagged a couple of times and fell over, bounced off the table and onto the floor. When I didn't come around Ricky and another friend loaded me into a car and drove to the local hospital.

They yelled at an orderly to bring a wheel chair and the three of them got me into the emergency room. They told the attendant I had overdosed on heroin and when he went to get help they split. So I was logged in as a "John Doe" and was treated with Naloxone, to counteract the effects of opiate overdose.

Had it not been for Ricky's quick thinking I could well have died that night. But overdosing didn't scare me like it should have. It didn't even slow me down. I never gave the hospital my real name and they had released me as soon as I was stable enough to walk without falling over. I called Joanne from a pay phone in the lobby and she came to the hospital and picked me up. Two hours later I was back at the apartment on Hastings Hill Road with a needle in my arm.

I was addicted to heroin and nothing short of death would keep me from the comfort of my next shot. I've heard it said that addicts were selfish, self-centered people who are afraid of life. Truth is junkies are fearless in the face of death. They live a life that is different from what normal people ex-perience and they embrace the possibility of death with each shot knowing full well that this shot, the one they were currently doing, may be their last. It takes balls to shoot heroin on a daily basis and my return to the needle after each overdose is living proof of this truth.

Chapter 15

Ultimately, the use of heroin fractured my group of friends between users and those who didn't want to be around it. As it turns out I was the heroin animated monster in their midst. Maybe it was fear, maybe disgust, or maybe it was fate. I don't know. I didn't care. The golden eye had me firmly in its grasp and I was simply, positively, absolutely in love with it. The truth is, life moves on, like a raging river, and it pretty much carries everybody with it.

Some drifted away fast, while others moved a bit more slowly, but there for a brief moment, we all seemed to be going in the same general direction. Maybe I noticed our little group changing and maybe I didn't. Maybe I accepted its unraveling as a natural development. We had always been pretty fluid. Truth was I didn't care. Those who didn't want to do heroin could go their own way; no harm no foul.

Danny, and his girlfriend Kim, were the first to distance themselves from those in our group who were using heroin. Different couples rented apartments based upon their friendship, romance or drug choice. Because of its centralized location our apartment became the hub of all drug activities. When it was all said and done we ended up with four apartments we could move between depending on what drug you were doing or who you wanted to hang out with. But having several apartments didn't provide absolute protection and it wasn't long before the law started nipping at our heels.

Our first hint of this unwanted attention came when Randy got busted bringing a large amount of MDA from Raleigh back to Clemmons. This didn't just happen. The SBI had figured Randy out and that put Ricky in danger. Randy's bond was high and it took him several weeks to get the money together and find a bondsman that would bail him out of jail.

By the time he managed to get out, Donna had left town and we never saw her again. I guess her fear of being associated with Randy and spending time in jail over a drug bust was greater than any love she had for him or their friends. I truly think this was probably the smartest life decision she ever made.

Our second hint that local law officials were looking at us came in the form of a social services raid on one of our party apartments. In the process of setting up a substantial drug ring Ricky and I had helped several people get apartments and on of these couples Joanne and Cliff. Ricky brought Cliff into the equation and Danny and I knew Joanne from our days at Universal Fabric.

Joanne had custody of two young boys from her first marriage, and she was a very good mother. But as with most divorces there was tension between Joanne and her ex-husband who had caught wind of our lifestyle and had brought social services into the equation. Luckily, the sheriff officers who came to the apartment with the social workers on their welfare check found nothing to suggest illegal drug activity.

It was an incredibly lucky break. It's hard to imagine how one of our major drug hubs could have been so clean. They had come expecting to bust us for any number of drugs however they found nothing. No baggies, no rigs, no bent up spoons. Nothing. Just a few beers in the refrigerator. I have always felt like this was an overstatement of the facts by Joanne's ex-husband.

But, there was not enough food in the apartment to feed two growing boys, the place smelled like an ashtray and needed a good cleaning. The furniture was not the best and black out shades were nailed over each window making the place as dark as a tomb. The boys had their own room, as well as their own beds, however they were not as clean as they should have been. They had few clothes and they had outgrown the ones they were wearing.

This was enough for social services to determine that the environment was unsafe for young children and that was enough for Joanne's ex-husband to win temporary, full-time custody of the boys. This would become a long, drawn out legal fight between Joanne and her ex-husband. To help her case Joanne left Cliff and moved back in with her parents. This move worked in her favor. For a time she chose clean living for the sake of her children and in the end she got shared custody of her kids.

Chapter 16

Meanwhile, because of Randy's run-in with the law and his subsequent legal woes, the task of bringing MDA into town fell to Ricky and me. Ricky knew the source and how the business worked so the fact that I took Randy's place was no big deal. The money was incredible. I had no idea you could make so much cash in so little time. Because of my time at Reynolds I was accustomed to large pay checks so naturally I viewed the massive amounts of money we made running MDA as a definite win. We kept the local supply high and the dope almost pure which pleased our customers and we used the profits to live our heroin based lives.

Food was the last thing on the list and after a year of non-stop heroin abuse I looked like I had just been just been released from a concentration camp. By the time I turned twenty I had dropped a good twenty pounds, to somewhere in the neighborhood of one-hundred and fifty pounds. I should have weighed in at around one-seventy to one-ninety. The effect of heroin on my health was beginning to show.

Most days I ate very little if anything at all. Maybe a hamburger and fries or an apple turnover, maybe a bacon, egg and cheese biscuit. Otherwise I lived on cigarettes, vodka and heroin. I was trapped between misery and madness and it was this way – the same way – day in and day out. It seemed like I spent all my time coming down from my last fix or fixing my next high. There was no letting up.

In the morning I would wake up sick so the first thing I did was stumble into my first fix of the day. Get a little heroin and a little water melting in my spoon. Cook it just right, one quick boil, and turn it into a spoonful of beautiful brown tablespoon of Black Tar that looked exactly like a golden eye.

Humanizing something as dangerous as heroin with an inference of that magnitude is just asking for trouble. Only the mind of a junkie would make such a connection. It's a love that was never meant to be.

Draw fresh cooked heroin into my rig, thump the air out, find my best vein and quieten the demand. Feel the poison pushing me higher and higher as I milked my morning fix, finish it off with one last push and then clean everything up. I could ride that high for an hour or two. Sometimes it would take hours for that first hit of the day to fade away. Once I had satisfied the craving, I could sit back and watch the remains of my last cook dry up and turned to a dark brown crust in the bottom of my spoon.

With every shot heroin extracted life from my frail body and I was so in love with the buzz that I didn't care. Most of the time just knowing I had heroin and a working rig was all I needed to have a descent day. I would set there in the dark, in that near empty apartment, shooting smack. I was blinded by my addiction and always scrambling for more; looking for a way to make the next shot my best shot.

I didn't just want to get well, I wanted to get high – as high as I dared and then some. This was going to end badly and I think I knew it. I rarely had company. The crash pad of Keith's days had dried up after a couple of nasty fights. We didn't call the cops because of extenuating circumstances but we made it clear that the participants were no longer welcomed at the Hastings Hill Road apartment.

Chapter 17

Most days I didn't talk to anyone. Ricky came and went, bringing food, vodka, cigarettes, rigs and more heroin. He was the only person I knew who could walk into a drugstore, tell the pharmacist he needed a two week supply of U-100 insulin syringes and actually get them. He looked the part.

Heroin was tearing me down, but Ricky looked innocent, fresh and young, healthy and honest and we used this unique mix and his ability to play it cool to get what we needed. We hit every drugstore in the city buying rigs. At one point we easily had two years of U-100 insulin syringes safely stashed away and ready to be used. And Ricky didn't mind doing the running for the crap that made our days livable.

So most of the time it was just me and heroin in the Hasting Hills Road apartment. And then there was our MDA business. I became the "cut man." Ricky would bring in a fresh quarter pound of MDA and I would sit there for hours, stepping on it a little bit, but keeping its purity intact. Then I weighed it out. Gram after gram. It was tedious, tiring work, but it had to be done and I was better at using a pair of triple beam scales than Ricky was so preparing the MDA for sell became my job.

This put me in a unique position. I had to be high on heroin to do anything, and you must have steady hands to cut dope. You'd also be foolish to think that while doing my job I wasn't sampling the drug I had to sit there and cut into grams. Multiple drug intoxication. With the heroin and MDA became too much for me to handle I took a Quaalude and evened myself out.

I spent hours a day doing this work and it got to the point I needed glasses just to see the pointer on the scales. I had to be accurate so I went and got glasses. You'd be surprised at the buyers who carry their own scales just to make sure their not being ripped off. To make sure they were always happy with me I added a pinch to every gram making them weigh heavy and that made me a very trusted dealer.

Chapter 18

When there was no MDA to cut I was left to my own devices. Nobody would believe the shit that went on inside my head. I sat in that darkened apartment all day long, nodding from fix to fix. I didn't like looking at myself in the mirror because it looked like I was evaporating. I got thinner and thinner with every glance. I looked like death warmed over. Everything seemed to be going fast and slow at the same time. Why did I feel like I would have to do my living after my dying?

I tried to make one-hundred dollars worth of heroin last all day. That was two bindles. But most of the time I couldn't. Two-hundred and fifty, or five bindles, was more like it. The problem with shooting that much dope is that you start running out of veins. Some veins become so callused that your needle won't penetrate them. They roll around under your skin as if they were dancing to keep away from the needle.

Preferred veins were overused and would often collapse, which meant they disappeared. I missed these veins the most and to find them I had to go deep. But that was painful and digging around in your arm didn't always guarantee that you would find a missing vein. Shooting heroin made a mess of my arms.

Damaged veins bled under my skin to produce massive, multicolored bruises. It was not uncommon for my entire left arm to be covered in wicked looking tracks. I was right handed, which meant that I had to shoot into my left arm and the top of my left hand. Top side tracks were the worst. It was hard to follow veins on the top side of my hand past my wrist. They went deeper and deeper until they disappeared.

When I couldn't find a vein on any part of my left arm

Ricky would have to administer my next hit and when he wielded the syringe we always hit veins in my right arm. Ricky was around each day enough to stay high so we split the heroin and helped each other get off. I would make sure he got off cleanly and he would do the same for me. Looking back I can honestly say that despite his good luck and devil may care attitude, Ricky was a very dangerous person to hang out with.

He was the common denominator in all of these situations. From trafficking, to dealing, to using. He loved shooting drugs and it didn't matter what is was; MDA, cocaine or heroin, all of which could be deadly if you didn't know where to draw the line. Around Ricky that line blurred all the time.

In a way I think Ricky felt like he was invincible. Occasionally I would ride with him and I didn't think twice about riding around high. Why should I care, I wasn't driving. The junk we loved and spent our days craving would make you crazy and that kind of crazy would get you killed.

He did have one frustrating habit that never failed to get on my nerves. He would bring stray junkies home without notice. If they were holding and weren't planning to stay that was tolerable. But if they were broke and didn't have any drugs I ran them off. I figured if they had money they would have dope and if they didn't, they were looking for a handout. I sure as hell wasn't sharing mine and I had told Ricky to stop this stupid shit on several occasions.

One day he brought home a guy named Went Dillinger. I recognized my personal demons' as well as Ricky's but Went was straight from hell. He had money, cocaine, heroin, rigs, marijuana and an endless variety of pills. And he didn't mind sharing what he had. Went was the first person I ever saw mix coke and heroin in the traditional "speed ball" form and trust you me that is one scary fucking scene.

I had scared myself a time or two over my relatively short exposure to heroin but Went was over the top. He could never get enough and verbally dared full rigs of heroin to kill him. I have never seen another human dance with the devil as skillfully as he did. He was an intense, explosive demonstration of drug fueled, human insanity. One day he commanded center stage and rioted without restraint.

The next day he was gone and we never saw him again. Later we heard that he had overdosed in one of Winston Salem's shooting galleries and died. When I thought about that I was relieved. Went had been one scary dude and I was glad he hadn't died in our apartment. Maybe that was selfish, maybe I was trying to protect my opium den from his over the top behavior. Truthfully I was glad Went was gone. He had the ability to bring a lot of bad karma to a situation that could not stand any more bad karma.

Chapter 19

Of course the idea of working a real job went out the window. If it hadn't been for dealing MDA at the level we were dealing it I would have probably returned to Yadkinville broke and addicted. But there were just to many detracting factors for that to happen. For one Ricky upped our game by bringing in larger loads of MDA. In a matter of months we doubled our output. This put us at the top of the local drug scene. Business was great and ours was no small business. Three times a month we purchased a quarter pound of MDA, stepped on it and cut it into grams.

We would then ride around selling MDA to all our friends. As it turns out we had a lot of friends. We could sell out in a week maybe less and were quick to return to Raleigh for more MDA. We were now supplying our regular customers and through word of mouth started picking up new ones. However, dealing to people you didn't know can be a dangerous business. Most of the time we didn't know our new customers as well as we knew our old ones. The old customers may vouch for new customers but they were still strangers and with strangers came dangers.

In fact, an increasing number of new customers were junkies we found in local shooting galleries. I don't remember exactly how we got involved in supplying junkies with MDA, however once we did our business mushroomed. Going into shooting galleries without protection could be a very dangerous. You had to buy protection from the shooting galleries owner and we paid cold hard cash to have his bodyguards protect us while we were on his property.

Chapter 20

But there were other dangers as well. It's dangerous to sell drugs to someone you didn't know and let me show you why. One day I got a call from a friend of a friend who said he had a friend who wanted to buy some MDA. If he like the quality he would buy more. I said fine and took a gram to meet this new customer. I had no way of knowing that this new friend was an undercover SBI agent or that the "friend" who had called me had been busted and was willing to sell me out for a lighter sentence.

The deal had went down as planned. I took one gram to my "friends" house, met the "new friend" and sold him a gram of MDA. I was somewhat surprised when this "new friend" didn't bother sampling it, yet immediately wanted more. Something about that just wasn't right, but I was too distracted by heroin to pay these types of transactions the attention they deserved.

I was in my home county so I felt like I was in my comfort zone and that everybody was cool. When he offered me five hundred dollars up front for an ounce I should have known something was not quiet right. In the drug business everything is done for the cash and nobody fronts anybody anything. His willingness to front me five-hundred dollars should have tipped me off but I said okay and left with five hundred of the state's dollars and a promise to be back in a couple of hours.

On my way back to Clemmons my car broke down. This left me on the side of the road. I'm not an auto mechanic so I turned toward home, ready to walk the last few miles, when Cliff and Ricky happened to drive by. They were going to the beach and asked if I wanted to tag along. I said "sure" and spent a few minutes sanitizing my car of anything incriminating, including my license plate. I then got into their car and we stopped by Hasting Hills Road long enough to grab my heroin and its essentials.

The three of us spent the next two weeks at the beach enjoying the atmosphere and partying. I shot all my heroin and spent all my money, including the state's five hundred dollars. I forgot about the deal I had made with the SBI three weeks earlier. We returned to North Carolina and Ricky and I returned to the drug business. We bought another car because my old car had disappeared. Once we had a new car we traveled to Raleigh for our next quarter pound and went back to business as usual.

Step on it, cut it into grams and satisfy both our MDA customers as well as our own need for heroin. Our profit on that quarter pound was so great we weren't in any rush to do it again. We paid the rent and settled into a month's worth of heroin abuse. We nodded, slept and woke up to do it all over again. It didn't take long for our heroin needs to require a run and everything went perfectly. Our method of operation was simple and productive. The only dicey part of our business was the shooting galleries.

And then there was the heroin. A lot of times we found heroin in the shooting galleries and would work out a MDA – heroin trade for as much as the other dealers were willing to part with. I would often stay in a gallery just long enough to fix myself a rig full. I would shoot part of it there and save the rest for later. As Ricky drove us from sell to sell I sat in the passenger seat milking blood.

Ricky never missed an opportunity to get high and looking back I'm amazed he didn't wrap us around a power pole or drive us into oncoming traffic. When I think about all the crazy things we did it seems like, in many ways, Ricky and I were living as though we were already dead. Even if you don't take the possibility of accidental overdose into account, this lifestyle would wear you thin.

Chapter 20

This brings me back to the subject of dealing drugs. At one point I think it would be safe to say that we had between two and three-hundred customers buying MDA from us on a weekly basis. We made a substantial profit from every run and since you couldn't put drug money in the bank we ended up with trash bags full of cash. Cash you own but can't go out and spend. Of course we used it to live on, to purchase the drugs we sold and did, and we used some of it to buy a used Jeep Cherokee we found in Auto Trader. Several months later we splurged and bought a brand new 1982 Chevy Malibu Classic.

If anyone was watching, these purchases would have definitely raised a red flag. We had more money than sense and as it turns out the SBI was watching us very closely. I might have forgotten about the five hundred dollars they had fronted me to buy an ounce of MDA but they had not forgotten me. They could have filed charges for the one gram of MDA that I had sold to their undercover agent and the five hundred dollars that I had basically stolen from them. However, they were more interested in where we were getting our MDA and looking back I feel pretty sure they were monitoring our every move.

They wanted to arrest the man at the top and take the drug ring down piece at a time, starting with us and moving up. They won't get to, but that didn't keep them from trying. Perhaps the main reason they had such a hard time catching us was because we were always on the move. We never got rid of the Hasting Hills Road apartment and we didn't need a lot to live this new version of our chosen lifestyle. We traveled lite. It was an angle. We could be here, there, or just about anywhere.

In fact, the only things our mobility required was a back pack and a sleeping bag. The contents of our back packs were very revealing. Clothes, drugs, as much cash as we could carry, and paraphernalia. We willingly lived like street urchins. We were front and center at most parties and a lot of times it was our drugs that kept the party going.

Another phenomenon specific to this period in time was outdoor rock concerts. It was like a miniature Woodstock. Local bands such as Nantucket, The Brotherhood of Peace, Great White and other lesser known bands came together, in the middle of a field, and had a Friday to Sunday music festival. A lot of times the bands had to use diesel powered generators for electricity. So imagine music so loud you couldn't hear the generators and you have an idea of how loud these concerts were.

Of course these events were not without their peril. You had to be ready to move at a minutes notice and this was generally one very basic reason. People with very little drug experience were always overdosing and in need a emergency medical care, which always came to the concert in the form of ambulances. If this happened the cops were not far behind so we left when we started hearing sirens.

Truthfully we enjoyed the party. We were keen to pick up drugs we were unfamiliar with, do a pinch here and there, just to see what were dealing it. I think my favorite one time drug experience was Hash. I have long wished for more but it's just not available in my neck of the woods. It might sound crazy but during this period I didn't need a bed. I slept in my clothes, in my sleeping bag, in the Jeep, whose back seats could be laid down and were perfect for our type of vagrancy.

We moved from town to town, county to county. Sometimes we rented apartments, sometimes a mobile home and sometimes a house. The location didn't really matter so long as it was new, out of the way and unpredictable. We changed our phone number on a regular basis. Sometimes we put it in Ricky's name and sometimes we put it in mine. It was always unlisted. Sometimes, for a premium, we would put the power and phone in a friend's name. This was our safest bet and I preferred it above all others.

Sometimes we took our money and heroin and rented a condo at the beach. We completely disappeared for weeks at a time. When we ran low on money we returned from the underground, bought a quarter pound of MDA, stepped on it and spent days measuring out grams for our retail business. We then rode around with a couple hundred grams of MDA at a time, selling our friends whatever they wanted. We finished each round selling to junkies in shooting galleries.

Once our customers were satisfied we would buy as much heroin as we needed for a couple weeks and hole up somewhere. Sometimes we just wanted more money so we would up our trips to Raleigh to one a week. Maybe we wanted to take a couple girls on a cruise or indulge in an extended stay at the beach. Or hold an invitation only party on the top the Piedmont Building, where the steaks were perfect and the vodka flowed non-stop. These were not cheap events but they brought our closest friends together for a party you couldn't find anywhere else.

We would then return to Raleigh and repeat the cycle. This kept our customer base high while at the same time flying below the radar of local law enforcement. We also had to keep up with our shooting gallery business and this could be tricky because they moved about as frequently as we did. Galleries changed hands and all to often they moved without notice which meant trolling the streets looking for junkies who could tell us where the new galleries were.

Chapter 22

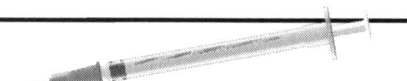

But sometimes you just lost a gallery. That's the way it was. People got busted and couldn't get out of jail. Junkies overdosed and died which always brought the cops. I've seen junkies watch their fellow junkie die just so they could steal what remained in the bottom of their dead buddy's spoon. That kind of shit happened a lot more than you might think. At first it was shocking to watch but eventually you learned how to block it out of your mind.

It was all an angle and a lot of times crowded shooting galleries were deliberately moved so that only the junkies and dealers knew where they were. If they left us out of the loop it may take weeks to find the new galleries. The ugly truth was these shooting galleries had became a good half of our business and so we had to do whatever was necessary to find them.

There's another unfortunate consequence that comes from dealing drugs for a living. When Randy got busted he became too hot to be around and suddenly he found himself in no-man's land. Desperate for a fix and not knowing his way around the street level drug market like Ricky and I did, he devised a very stupid plan. He decided to rob a drugstore. He was looking for any narcotic he could find.

He managed to score a small amount of drugs however his get away plan was seriously flawed and he was quickly arrested. This time his bail was set so high that he couldn't get out of jail on his own and nobody he knew would help him out. When you're running drugs for a living you don't associate with someone in trouble on drug related offensives because that could bring the law down on you.

In addition your "friend" might turn on you just to make their case easier and that happens more than you might think. So Randy was hung out to dry and forgotten. It may seem cold but that's how it works. He was on his own and looking back I can't even say what happened to him. With the felonies he was facing he probably did a long stretch in prison but truthfully I don't remember. And I don't care. That's how drugs work on the professional level.

Some people stick around until they wake up and choose sobriety thereby saving their lives. Others lose everything they own and are forced out simply because they can no longer afford their addiction. Some people get busted and end up in jail, where you sober up fast, while others die by overdose. That's just the nature of the game. And trust me if you dare consider trafficking illegal drugs a game, you better understand that it's a deadly game. Especially if personal addiction is part of the equation.

To insulate ourselves from anything Randy might say or do, Ricky and I moved so frequently that we stopped renting houses or apartments and for a good year rented hotel rooms in and around the Winston Salem area. We continued selling MDA and doing heroin and anytime we felt like something was not quite right we packed up and moved to another hotel. Maybe we were just paranoid and maybe we were hyper vigilant. Either way this mode of operation kept us from getting busted and allowed us to come and go without being noticed by law enforcement.

Chapter 23

Ricky was the first of my personal friends to die. He drove through a four-way stop at fifty miles an hour and was t-boned by a full size four-wheel drive pick-up. Both vehicles were completely destroyed. The scene was horrific. Our new Chevy Malibu was ripped in half and thrown sideways a good fifteen-hundred yards. It caught the side of the road and flipped, end over end, three times. Ricky was not wearing his seat-belt and was thrown from the car. Its first flip threw him through the windshield, its second flip crushed him, killing him instantly, and the final roll rocked backward and landed on him.

I'm not sure what Ricky was doing that day but the investigating cops found drugs and money in the car. No surprise there. The fact that I was not in the car was just plain luck and the fact that the car was registered in Ricky's name, was also just luck.

Around thirty people attended Ricky's funeral that Friday and I knew everyone that showed up except two dark suited men who slid in just as the ceremony was beginning and left just before the grave side service was over. I would later learn that these two strangers were SBI agents who attended the funeral seeking proof of Ricky's death. They also wanted to get a look at his friends who they assumed were all either drug dealers or drug addicts.

They could not have been more wrong. The only people who attended Ricky's funeral were members of his family. His friends understood the rules so the word went around and the next day Ricky's friends all met in the private suite of a local restaurant and had a party in his honor. Good food and friends. All the cocaine and alcohol we could consume. I covered the check as my way of paying tribute to a good guy, who was a good friend and who, like the rest of us, lived on the wrong side of the law.

Chapter 24

Ricky's death put an end to my drug trafficking days. No one stepped up to join me and I didn't want to do it on my own. Truth was, I felt that it was time to stop trafficking drugs and kick my heroin habit before I got arrested or died of an overdose. I stopped selling MDA the day of his funeral. But I knew where to score heroin and truthfully I knew that I could not just walk away from it. Its hooks were in me and I knew quitting would definitely hurt.

I don't know that I mourned Ricky's death in the traditional sense. Melinda's death by motor vehicle had cracked my brain and now here was Ricky, dead by the same measure. To this day I have a fear of cars that will not go away. The death of loved ones was very hard on me and I turned to a non-stop inflow of drugs to keep myself numb, twenty-four hours a day, seven days a week. I missed Ricky because with him around the party never stopped and in his absence it came to a screeching halt.

But I found myself sitting on thousands of dollars of drug money, all profits from the past two years of MDA sales. There was shoe boxes and trash bags full of cash. So I went underground and embarked on twelve months of thoughtless, mind melting heroin abuse. There was no furniture in the back bedroom of Hasting Hills Road, so I propped myself up in a corner of the room and shot smack non-stop.

My world evolved around a plate, a large spoon, a candle, and as many fresh rigs as I could come up with. Only the hardiest driven junkies beat a path to my door. As a result I did not always have to go out in search of junk. There were plenty of times when it found its way to me. I sat there in the bedroom of that apartment, with a needle and a spoon, and let heroin take my life away.

Chapter 25

During this twelve month period I overdosed three times, but each time, for some reason, I didn't die. I somehow made it through. For a junkie, three years in the making, that's saying a lot. But without fresh cash the money I was sitting on began to run low. My habit had ballooned to three-hundred dollars a day and to keep myself from running out I had to start stretching my purchases. But I ran out of money and when I did the parasites stopped coming around.

That meant I had to go in search of my own smack. I was now on my own, struggling for every dollar I could beg or borrow to score heroin. I became more and more desperate. I couldn't go back to dealing because I didn't know the main man or have the cash to get started. During this period every fix came at great expense and there were times when a partially filled rig looked like a bullet in the chamber of a gun, waiting to be fired into my brain. I was desperate. A self inflicted murder waiting to happen.

I was in bad shape however it was nobodies fault but mine. I was the dealer and the addict. I saw heroin from both sides and I knew that addiction is repetition. Dealers count on that. Repeating heroin is nasty. I sat in the corner with a rig in my arm and milked blood for hours at a time. I shot vodka just to have something to shoot. Over a period of several weeks I began to slowly wrap my wasted, inebriated mind around the fact that if I didn't stop shooting heroin I was going to die.

It took me months to claw my way back from the edge of drug induced insanity. The golden eye had guided me to the brink of self destruction and when I quit shooting heroin it had left me there to find my way home as best I could. The months following this decision were horrible. For the first couple of weeks I was so fragile it felt like I could crumble into a billion pieces. The pain of withdrawal twisted my stomach into agonizing knots that lasted for days. It was like shock therapy for my entire body.

I sat there alone in that miserable apartment with nothing but vodka and cigarettes and hallucinated bugs crawling all over me, all over the floor, all over the walls. I lived in the dark, on my own and nobody cared whether I lived or died. I was sure someone would come by to check on me. But nobody did and I lay there on my own. Apparently my friends had forgotten me and my fellow junkies had found somewhere else to go. It was bad, that much is true, but still, it's no way to treat the living dead.

Every inch of my skin crawled. It felt like I was suspended above a thorn-covered conveyor belt and when it moved the thorns would dig into my skin ripping it to shreds. The sensation was like being skinned alive. With each lurching forward of my phantom conveyor belt, more and more of my skin was torn from my body. The pain was unreal. Every nerve was on fire. There was no relief. Suicide was my only escape and I didn't have enough of anything to make it happen. So I was left to endure the tortures of withdrawal, sober and alone.

Another wicked side effect of withdrawal was sleep, or should I say the lack thereof. I would doze off for a few minutes and be jerked awake as if I had been electrocuted. I would then stay up for days only to take an unexpected nap and then stay up for several more days thinking about that nap. I would drive around to everyone I knew looking for sleeping pills, pain pills, nerve pills. Anything that would help me off the razor's edge. Once I had scored enough to matter I would return to the apartment and mix them with near lethal amounts of vodka. I was in a real bind and I knew it.

Chapter 26

I was running out of money so I had to get drug free quick if I hoped to get a job. But weeks passed and every day I lay on my sleeping bag quaking inside. I wanted my job at Reynolds back but I had to get clean and strong enough to make it through the inter-view process. I also knew that part of that process was a drug test. I was also aware of the fact that I did not look like the healthiest specimen. I had failed to eat properly over the past three years and I desperately needed to gain some weight.

So I started eating. Whatever I could afford, as much as I could consume. After a month of gorging on high-fat, fast food, I had gained twenty pounds and while I needed to gain more I was looking better. If you didn't look at my tracked scarred arms you would say that I was fairly fit and ready for work. Time passed and I successfully stayed away from everything but alcohol and sleeping pills.

One night, the sandman filled my eyes with sleep and for the first time in years I went to bed sober and slept until dawn. I slept good for the next several nights and after a couple weeks of this I went to Reynolds and applied for my old job. Several days later, Reynolds called and after an interview, drug test included, I went back to work. This return to work was a celebration of my successful struggle to kick heroin and return to a sober life and it occurred sometime around my twenty-second birthday.

I should have ran with this rare opportunity because it was as good as it was going to get. But I was young and foolish and I had celebrated my first paycheck by purchasing a single bindle of heroin and shooting a couple of rounds. That's all it took. I had ended a three year addiction by kicking heroin out of my life – an effort that required three months – and now I had opened the door and invited it back into my life. It readily accepted my invitation and enslaved me once again.

Having a job allowed me to acquire smack whenever I wanted it, which was weekly. I bought large amounts of the stuff because my greatest fear was running out. I had access to the drug supermarket found in Reynolds parking lot, but truthfully all I wanted was smack. I knew I had to take it slow for the sake of my arms and I did manage to slow my use to one hit in the morning and another at night.

But I never truly got heroin out of my life and it had no plans for turning me loose. I couldn't function without it and it needed a body to poison. I had a job so all I had to do was focus on it and everything else would take care of itself. I moved from the apartment on Hasting Hills Road and broke all ties to the MDA crowd. Once I had successfully broke those ties I came out of hiding by moving again.

The only connections I kept were the ones I needed for my drugs. Heroin had blurred large segments of my memory and I simply forgot most people. I had stayed strung out so long that when some random memory bubbled to the surface it would hopelessly drown when I tried focusing on it. Smack had taken an erasure to my brain and I could not remember much of what had happened the past three years.

I seemed blessed with a case of paranoia and was forever looking over my shoulder. I avoided everyone and as it turned out this was not very hard because my customers had went and found new connections. As a result, my MDA customer base slipped away like early morning fog. I didn't realize what a spider web Ricky and I had woven until I watched it fall apart. However once it had, I felt free.

Selling drugs was a part of my past, not my future and there was no point in dwelling on it. All I needed was my heroin connection. Over time my memory did improve and eventually I reached a point I like to call selective amnesia. I didn't want to remember everything and I hated the things I did remember. Like the fact that I was a heroin addict or that my mind saw a tablespoon of freshly cooked smack as a beautiful golden eye; staring up at me – waiting for me. But it wasn't an eye. It was an addiction.

Chapter 27

While I was thinking about my future, the past came calling. Even though I had forgotten them, the SBI had not forgotten me. They hadn't been able to increase the number of drug charges they had on me because they hadn't been able to get close to either me or Ricky. They had tried on numerous occasions to track us down but in the end all they had was the purchase of one gram of MDA and the five hundred dollars of their money that I had kept.

The SBI felt like they had been outsmarted and they were naturally infuriated. They planned to arrest me the night we set up the deal and had staked out my "friends" house prepared to do just that. But I had never returned. I had walked away with their money and car trouble, followed by the beach trip, followed by the fact that I just forgot them, kept me from returning with their drugs.

I was more consumed by my world than I was affected by theirs. Of course they thought I had ripped them off on purpose so naturally they were furious. Truth was I had planned to return with the drugs, however events beyond my control prevented that from happening. I had then went to the beach and when Ricky and I got back we went underground so they never got another chance to arrest me.

When I went back to work I came out of hiding feeling like a free man. I felt like I had gotten away with two years of drug trafficking and since three years of heroin use hadn't killed me I felt pretty lucky. However, trafficking MDA had elevated me and Ricky to the top of the SBI's ten most wanted list. Ricky had been marked off the list when his death had been verified and when I came out of hiding it did not take long for them to get a bead on me.

I'm not sure if this helped or hurt but I needed a slower, cleaner environment so instead of staying in Clemmons, where the drugs flowed freely and everybody knew me, I moved a fourth time. This time I moved back to Yadkinville, back to my hometown. Back to where it all began. To where very few people knew me. Life was slower in Yadkinville, cleaner some might say, and I was hoping to relax into a normal life.

On the down side, my left arm was in bad shape. I bore the scars of an active intravenous drug user and to cover them I always wore long sleeves, even in the Summer. I'm not sure if my parents realized what I had been through the past four years. If they knew they didn't say anything and I was able to continue shooting heroin. I stored all my drug shooting paraphernalia among a collection of shoe boxes beneath my bed. I reasoned that this was as good a hiding place as any. Unless of course I got busted.

Each morning my mother woke me up with a hearty breakfast and she always sent me to work with more food than I could eat. This attention to my health helped me regain even more weight. Maybe they knew more than I gave them credit for and were trying to nurse me back to health. Truth was I looked like I had aged a good twenty years and my daily withdrawal symptoms were down right scary.

However I managed to kept my "jonesing" to a minimum which meant my heroin use slowed to a crawl. Just enough to get by. As time passed I got stronger. I continued gaining weight and steadily put more and more space between heroin and myself. I began helping out around the place, mowing the yard, working in the garden. Chores that surprisingly kept my mind off drugs.

Chapter 28

One particular Saturday afternoon I was off work and sitting on the back porch swing enjoying the day. It was mid-Summer and the temperature, humidity readings were almost tropical. I could not help but notice that there were a large number of police cars circling the block. I walked around the corner of the house and saw cops parked on the side of the road in all directions. Town cops, sheriff deputies, highway patrol and unmarked cars.

This time the SBI was coordinating resources that stretched across several law enforcement agencies and escape was not going to be easy. When I felt them closing in I tried to get out of town. Five miles in either direction and I would have easily escaped however I needed gas and had stopped at the last gas station in town for a quick fill up. I never made it out of the parking lot.

Cops came from all directions and boxed me in at the gas pumps. They finally had me. After years of playing this cat and mouse game, after trying and failing repeatedly the SBI had finally taken down a top drug dealer. The fact that I had voluntarily retired from the drug business and came out of hiding on my own only made it easier for them to find me. I was charged with one count of possession with the intent to sell and one count of sale and delivery of a controlled substance.

Both charges stemmed from my lone encounter with the undercover SBI agent who had purchased one gram of MDA from me and nothing more. There was the question of the five-hundred dollars but that was a sticky subject and the SBI was not sure how to pro-ceed. So they went with the best they could hope for and since both charges were felonies the judge set my bond fairly high. However, my father had bailed me out of jail and the next day we hired the best lawyer Yadkinville had to offer.

It quickly became delightfully apparent that the SBI did not have much of a case. Yes, I had sold them one gram of MDA and yes their undercover agent had made a deal to purchase a lot more. However, he had broke SBI rules when he gave me five hundred dollars in advance of any drug deal. He had shot the SBI in the foot and I unwittingly punched a big hole in their case by not returning with the drugs.

After several "behind closed door" conversations with the participating actors my lawyer told me that the SBI would have to drop the "possession with intent to sell" charge because of a lack of evidence. All they had left was the "sell and delivery" charge and that reduced my felony count to one. The SBI was not happy with that but it was the best case they could bring before a judge.

In fact, while the SBI thought they had worked out a deal to keep their screw-ups out of court when it came time for my lawyer to present my defense he attacked the SBI. He let the judge know that the SBI had put the squeeze on another dealer to lure me from a neighboring county and I had never sold drugs while living in Yadkin County. All my drug activity had been in a neighboring county and that county did not even have a file on me.

Adding to this menagerie was the reigning sheriff who spoke to the judge on my behalf and described me as "a good ole' boy." When the SBI agent admitted to giving me money in advance of any delivery and then said that I had not returned with either cash or drugs, the judge actually chuckled. However, he quickly told my lawyer I would have to pay that back. I let my lawyer do his thing and in the end I was fined a couple thousand dollars and sentenced to six months in jail with unlimited work release.

Chapter 29

In other words, as long as I was working I didn't have to be in jail. I already worked at Reynolds ten hours a day so all I needed was a second job and I found one working on a family friend's tobacco farm. He didn't have to do anything but to keep me out of jail he put me to work plowing, cultivating and planting his tobacco crop. So I worked for him every morning. I was able to leave jail at 5AM and work from 6AM until noon plowing tobacco. With that six hours under my belt I would make a quick stop by my parents for a shower and some lunch.

Mom always sent me to work with a bag full of food and following my ten hour shift at Reynolds I returned to jail and slept from around 1AM until 5AM. I repeated this grueling schedule every day of the week except Sunday. Cool thing about the sheriff was that he let me out of jail Sunday morning to go to church provided I went with my parents. I had never cared much for church but it was better than jail, so I went. After four months of this exhausting pace he turned me loose for good behavior.

The best thing to come out of my four month stay in jail was that I finally kicked my heroin addiction and I am quick to credit the sheriff with going above and beyond his obligation. He didn't know it at the time but the way he treated me helped me get sober. I signed up for the local Methadone program and each day, on my way to work, I stopped by the clinic for the drug that was supposed to wean me off heroin. I had never put much faith in Methadone.

I had seen people use it when they couldn't find heroin and go back to heroin when became available again. But I was in jail so Methadone was as good as I could get. And it worked. I didn't suffer the pains of withdrawal and stayed enrolled in the program for a good year. The worst thing to come out of my four month stay in jail was the fact that during this period a number of friends died. First, Joanne died from a cocaine in-duced heart attack. Keith and his girlfriend were killed in a car wreck and Cliff was killed by a hit and run driver, walking down the road.

Chapter 30

I had survived an incredible ordeal and I didn't want to go back to a life of drugs so I began planning a different future for myself. I was ready to leave Yadkin County and I didn't want to continue working at Reynolds so I started looking for a job that would change my scenery. And I found one working for a company that took baby pictures in K-Mart. Everybody out there has seen this set up.

It was an unusual job to say the least, especially for me. Most people found it a hard job to do because it required one hundred percent travel. This meant exactly what it said: travel; seven days a week, all month long, every month of the year, all year long. There was no going home. Home was whatever hotel you were staying in, in whatever town you happened to be in, for that weeks shoot.

One shoot followed another with three days between each for travel and set up. Originally my territory was North Carolina, South Carolina and Virginia. However, I was frequently sent to Washington D.C., Delaware, Baltimore Maryland, Pennsylvania and New Jersey. This job got me about as far away from Yadkin County as I could get. The company paid all hotel bills, one-hundred percent logged miles, a bi-weekly salary, quarterly bonuses, a daily food allowance, seven paid holidays, five paid personal days, and two weeks paid vacation per year.

The money was great. I loved the freedom it brought to my life. I enjoyed being in a new town every week and living in hotels spoiled me rotten. Every day my bed was made with clean sheets and my room was thoroughly cleaned. Fresh towels and accessories were always left in the bathroom. My only requirement was that any hotel I stayed in, had to have, or be closely located to a working bar.

I was not that far away from my drug infested years and I had to be careful because if I started missing heroin I could have easily went back to that way of life. But I didn't. I drank myself to sleep every night and vodka became my only vice. Traveling non-stop became my saving grace. I didn't stay in one place long enough to make a connection and that was good for me because there is one fact I know to be true.

Once you're addicted, you're always an addict. You may choose your poison, but its your brain doing the craving, so the chemistry of addiction is always the same. Addiction will turn a seemingly innocent play thing into a monster. There can be no deviation, no sampling of any kind. You have to be vigilant, alert, forever on guard against the possibility of addiction – to anything, even people.

You can't quit until you try
You can't live until you die
You can't learn to tell the truth
Until you learn to lie

You can't breathe until you choke
You gotta laugh when you're the joke
There's nothing like a funeral
To make you feel alive

Just open your eyes
And see that life is beautiful
Will you swear on your life
That no one will cry at my funeral?

I know some things that you don't
I've done things that you won't
There's nothing like a trail of blood
To find your way back home

I was waiting for my hearse
What came next was so much worse
It took a funeral to make me feel alive

Sixx A.M. The Heroin Diaries: Life is Beautiful
Darren Jay Ashba, James Michael, Nikki Sixx
Lyrics © Downtown Music Publishing LLC
Warner Chappell Music Inc.
Sixx Gunner Music

Chapter 31

Pain is inevitable. Anger turned inward is depression. Keep your secrets in the shadows and you'll be sorry. A little pain is good for the soul. We've all heard psychological jargon that seeks to explain the lives we live or how we feel. And they all have their merits. But, let's sit psychology aside and talk about pain. There are two kinds of pain; emotional and physical. Physical pain is easy to see. Scraps, cuts, broken bones. In time they all heal and go away. You may never forget the experience that caused you physical pain but you instinctively know how to compartmentalize it. If it didn't kill you its a boo-boo. You will get better.

Emotional pain is just as real and it can be just as serious. Possibly more so. It can be just as deadly and life altering as physical pain and its not always that easy to see. People suffering with emotional pain are expert at wearing mask to hid the issue inflicting pain on them. Emotional pain is the leading cause of substance abuse and suicide. Most of the time it seems to come from out of nowhere and crashes into us when we least expect it. It proves to be a nasty surprise. All too often it hits below the belt. Like being cheated on by a trusted spouse or the sudden, unexpected death of someone close to you.

We hope it won't last or that we can grin and bear it. Our instinct is to grit our teeth, brace ourselves, fight our way through it and hope that in time it goes away. We can't wait for it to leave and we don't want it coming back. But we have to deal with it. You can't avoid pain. You can't hide from it and you can't outrun it and you need to learn how to deal with it in a healthy manner because there's always more where that came from.

And it doesn't do any good to build walls. I knew that before laying my first mental block. Walls don't keep pain out, they just keep you in. To make matters worse, walls will cause you to lose your friends. To make matters worse the happy people don't want you around because their afraid they might catch what you've got. Rejection adds to the pain. We start denying it. We cover our pain with illusion and build monuments to our denial. We deny that we're in denial. We lie to ourselves so much that after a while the lie begins to feel like the truth. We lie so much that we don't recognize the truth, even when it's right in front of us. We ignore our mortality and focus on the frivolous, or worse we get dragged into the bowls of hell by an addiction we can't control.

Eventually our whole world becomes a series of illusions carefully placed to block out the pain. You can live like this for a while but you can't ignore the pain forever. Sometimes you have to work around it and then sometimes the pain is so huge it blocks out your life. The world you know fades to black. All that's real is the pain and how it makes you feel.

Vodka helps (no), nerve pills help (no), your friends will help (maybe). All they can really do is offer a shoulder to cry on, or lend a sympathetic ear. Sometimes they lighten your load. Sometimes it helps to talk it out and sometimes your friends leave you in the dark, alone. But then again, if you think about it, if you're in pain, the dark is a good place to be. In the dark you can sleep, relax, stop worrying about what everybody else thinks. In the dark there's hope for the light, there's faith in the light and a promise that one day the light will return and everything will get better.

Everybody needs to understand that there's a clear, undeniable line separating light and dark. It's a bold line and it's there for a reason. If you cross the line from light into dark you do so at our own peril. You forsake everything that makes your life make sense. If you foolishly trade light for dark you may find you can't trade back. You're stuck, hoping and praying you can find the line and cross back into the light before you go insane.

But with pain it doesn't matter. Pain can survive on either side of the line. It follows you no matter where you go. After a while you learn to make peace with it because you can't avoid it and you can't hide from it. Not even in the dark.

After a while you learn to take things in stride. You've lived with pain for so long that you know what it looks like and can actually see it coming. You learn to sidestep it. You get good at dodging it. You take your lessons to heart and apply them to your daily life. And then as if by magic, something amazing happens. You start to see the world differently. You don't hurt as much as you once did. When you least expect it you look up and notice that the pain is gone. It takes hard work, a keen eye and a little luck, but one day the Sun is shining, it stops raining and the pain melts away. That's the greatest feeling a body can have. It's as good as this life can offer. So when pain comes your way learn to recognize it, seize the day because seeing the beauty that life has to offer can be a rare event.

Chapter 32

Because I was willing to travel just about anywhere I got my choice of northern based shoots. I wanted to see the world but I settled for a meandering journey that took me through Washington D.C., and then Baltimore Maryland, on my way to Newark, Cherry Hill, Camden and finally Brooklawn New Jersey. From there I traveled north into the Poconos of Pennsylvania and then back to a town named Brick, on the New Jersey coast. I worked my way back down the east coast to the Del-Mar Peninsula and then back to the interior of Delaware. If you loved living on the road it would be hard to find a better job.

As for me, I was a southern country boy who was, on regular occasion, picked up and dropped into one of several northern states. I was young and handsome, unique and unusual. My southern accent was out of place and a delight to every female that came within ear shot. It is fair to say that I attracted a lot of attention and it is also fair to say that I enjoyed every minute of it.

But I had a secret. A secret that must be guarded at all times. A sleeping monster that I had to make sure never woke up. It was simple really. I was a twenty-three year old addict, less than one year away from a nasty three year heroin addiction and less than a year out of jail. But, nobody had to know this and I made sure that my drug soiled past was my best kept secret.

I had four relatively close shoots in New Jersey. Newark, Camden, Cherry Hill and Brooklawn. The first three had proven themselves to be busy shoots and my weeks in those towns passed rather quickly. Unfortunately Brooklawn had been painfully slow. The manager had set me up at the back of the store, in front of the deli and right beside the appliance department. I might as well have been invisible. I had a few customers but for the most part I just sat there waiting for mothers to bring me their babies.

So I resigned myself to a boring week and passed the time as best I could. Funny how the universe has a way of making sure you're exactly where you're supposed to be, at exactly the time you're supposed to be there. I used a "gone to lunch" and a "back in fifteen minutes" sign to explore the store. But I had to stay close to my photo gear because I didn't want anybody messing with it.

I was about to fall over dead from boredom when I got hit in the head by a well aimed rubber band. I looked around for my assailant and found myself staring into the eyes of the most beautiful woman I had ever seen. Never before had I known such beauty. She was an angel in the flesh, every inch of her was gorgeous; from her face and hair to her almond-shaped brown eyes and beautiful mouth. She was my age, she wanted to meet me and I was totally blown away by her attention.

Chapter 33

Her name was Melinda Marie, she lived right there in Brooklawn and she wanted to know everything about me. From where I grew up to what my job was like. We talked the week away. Any time neither of us had customers we could be found in the store's deli drinking coffee or the appliance department talking. Getting to know her was like dive bombing into a dream. By the end of the week I was in love; absolutely, positively, head over heels, in love. We traded addresses, the photo company would forward my mail to me every week along with fresh film, shoot schedules and any other relevant items.

Melinda and I arranged to talk to each other once or twice a week by phone. We had a designated time to call and I would simply call her from my hotel room. We talked for hours. About everything. Her life so near Philadelphia and mine as a southern farm boy. I left out the offending parts; like my addiction to heroin, the time I spent trafficking drugs, or the time I spent in jail paying off my debt to society.

I didn't want to lose contact with this precious, angelic person and since she initiated our relationship I was not going to ruin it with stories of an outlaw life. During the first couple months we communicated by telephone and mail because my schedule kept me in my original territory. At first this had been a pleasing territory. A lot of my shoots were along the beach and before meeting Melinda I had enjoyed working in my backyard. During the first several months of our relationship I had been satisfied with phone calls, post cards and letters. We were constantly surprising each other with small gifts.

It didn't have to be much or expensive, just unique and unexpected. Something to say; "I'm thinking of you." However, the better I got to know her the more I wanted to be close to her. So I applied for a transfer from the southeast division to the northeast division. I got my supervisor on the phone and told him exactly why I wanted to make the change and he promptly granted it. In fact, he had said that this type of situation was a perk of the job and that I could move just about anywhere so long as there was an empty position that needed filling.

My new territory was Delaware, New Jersey and the eastern third of Pennsylvania. This was perfect. Sometimes I could see Melinda several times a week. All I had to do was drive from my shoot location to Brooklawn and be back in time for the next day's business. I drove a lot at night and logged a lot of miles that I couldn't claim. But I didn't care. This was the one time in my life when insomnia actually worked in my favor. I would get up around six in the morning and go to bed around two or three the next morning. The chance of seeing Melinda for a few hours every other day or so was precious and these carefully planned encounters made the long hours worth it.

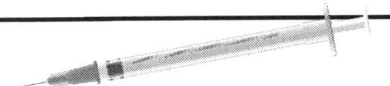

Chapter 34

Sometimes all we had time for was a later dinner or a long, leisurely walk in one of Brooklawn's many river side green ways. I remember how one of her favorite meals was a shrimp salad sandwich. The relationship we were developing was incredible. It was fast and slow at the same time. Within months we knew everything about each other, from our favorite wine, to our favorite movie and our favorite music. She had turned me on to The Moody Blues and I made sure my car carried every Moody Blues cassette I could find in the K-Mart music department.

Next I used my payroll and expense checks to rent an apartment right there in Melinda's neighborhood. When I showed her the apartment she was both surprised and excited. She walked from room to room as if imagining where every piece of furniture would go and checked out the view from every window. At first I didn't say anything about us living together, but I did ask her to help me decorate it and I gave her a key so that she could come and go as she pleased.

We then started furniture shopping. Sometimes together and sometimes she went alone. Melinda said that we would leave the bedroom alone for now and since this made her feel more comfortable with the whole idea I had said "no problem." But I could see that she clearly enjoyed being in that apartment. I say that because she was constantly decorating it, rearranging its furniture and working on a look that slowly began to gel. I kept her in spending cash so that she could buy anything she wanted and I never questioned her taste or any purchase she made.

Some furniture didn't turn out right and ended up in the bedroom as just a place to be, out of the way. I didn't say a word. She was clearly exploring something that was new and exciting for her. This was the first place that she could explore the art of using furniture to decorate different rooms and I must admit I was as excited as she was. She clearly had an idea of how she wanted the apartment to look and she kept working with the space until it slowly became a home.

Next I had a telephone installed so we could talk when I was on the road and she was at the apartment. I didn't say anything about the lack of a bed. For me it was enough to know that Melinda felt safe and comfortable in an apartment that was rapidly becoming ours. During the apartments formative months we spent our days off together, exploring Philadelphia and eating out. We were oh so adult. We drank wine at sidewalk cafes, smoked cigarettes and at the end of the day I would take her home. I would return to the apartment, sleep on the couch and give myself enough time to get to my shoot on time.

Chapter 35

One day Melinda invited me to eat lunch with her family that coming Sunday. I immediately said okay. It was the perfect opportunity to met her mom and brother and I looked forward to it because it meant she was inviting me into her inner circle. I don't know anything about her father. She never spoke of him and I never asked.

Lunch was great. Melinda and her mother were great cooks. Her brother was about my age and the four of us talked all afternoon. I told them everything there was to know about my job, where I was from and my family. By mid-afternoon lunch was over and Melinda and I were on our way to the apartment. On the way she had casually asked how I liked spending my nights at the apartment. I had said that "it was okay" but I complained that the couch was too soft for my back. I was waking up so sore and stiff that I was thinking about sleeping on the floor.

Melinda suddenly realized that I was willing to rent a place for us. We were spending most of our free time there and I had bought everything that she picked out for us. I hadn't said anything about how bad the couch slept until now but when she heard that I was thinking about sleeping on the floor just to get away from the pain and that I didn't even have a pillow she couldn't help but think that I was suffering because of her.

In her mind that would not do. I was lacking basic creature comforts and she was determined to put an end to it. So she directed me to a small neighborhood furniture store and we bought a double bed. This was a critical step along the path I believed would end with us living together. The next day the new bedroom furniture was delivered and set up. This gave Melinda a brand new room to decorate and we had started by buying sheets and pillars, a bedspread and a comforter.

We held hands a lot that day. It was as if we couldn't keep our hands off one another. We also purchased curtains and blinds, an alarm clock radio and a chest of drawers. The bedroom was complete and still Melinda chose to live with her mother. We never talked about her spending the night at the apartment. Pushing this beautiful woman in a way she wasn't ready for would have been wrong. So I let things be as Melinda wanted them to be.

However one evening while we were dining out she told me that tonight she would be staying with me. She had told her mother where she would be and her mother had given our relationship her seal of approval. This was the last piece of the puzzle. The doorway to true adulthood was finally in sight. As I thought back over the last eighteen months I couldn't help but marvel at how my life had changed. I had known Melinda for about six months and heroin hadn't crossed my mind once. With her by my side I would never think of it again.

Chapter 36

Our relationship changed that night. We became lovers. We might have fumbled about unaware and we might have failed to push all the right buttons, but we became lovers and that took our relationship to a new level. Neither one of us knew anymore about making love than the other but we were patient and gentle with each other. Being together had its own reward. Waking up together took our relationship to yet another level and watching the Sun rise while we enjoyed our morning coffee and cigarettes on the back deck confirmed the obvious. We were lovers in love; two adults in a committed relationship.

Our love was monumental, it was staggering, life changing and we knew it. We reveled in it, relived it in our memories and for that precious, fleeting moment, the possibilities seemed endless. I remember telling Melinda that the best feeling I had ever had in my life was being hundreds of miles away from her and still being able to see her face. It made me fee like we were always connected.

I told her it was a tremendous comfort knowing she was thinking of me and she had smiled effortlessly, realizing that we shared the same level of intimacy. I suddenly felt like I was so in love with her that if I couldn't live with her I couldn't live at all. Our newfound love was strong and true and for me it stood where there had once been absolutely nothing. I loved how that felt.

Chapter 37

Sunday and Monday were always my days off and on the days that Melinda was off, or after she got off work, we would go into Philadelphia so that I could see the city as the locals show it. We walked the same streets that Philly's infamous mobsters walked, ate at family restaurants that were decades old and took in all the sites. She wanted me to see how special her side of Philadelphia was but, in truth, when I was with Melinda I lost sight of everything but her.

She was mesmerizing and poetic. For me she was the word "beautiful" and she had an angelic, tender spirit that made her wise beyond her years. In my eyes she was the perfect blend of beauty and brains. I had never met anyone like her. She possessed a spirituality that seemed to be a blessing from the gods and even though our relationship was in its infancy it was growing day by day and I could see it lasting forever. We returned to the apartment and Melinda called her mother to let her know that she was okay.

We spent that evening at the apartment sipping champagne and snuggling on the couch. We didn't need a T.V., or a radio. We had each other and our love was all encompassing. It was so tangible that nothing else mattered. It was a glorious experience. One that I would treasure for a lifetime. The evening slowly slipped away and sometime after dark Melinda called her mother to tell her that tonight she would be staying with me. I would spend the night in the arms of an angel.

But Tuesday morning came soon enough and I had a five day shoot in Allentown Pennsylvania. As with all my other shoots it ran from Tuesday through Saturday with the plan being that I would leave very early Tuesday morning and be home by midnight Saturday. So I packed enough clothes for the week, woke Melinda to say good-bye and reminded her that I would call her later in the week. By the time I left the apartment she had went back to sleep. She was peaceful, safe and sound and that was, in and of itself, an incredibly satisfying feeling. During my absence she would stay at her mom's house but she had a key to the apartment so she could come and go as she saw fit.

Chapter 38

For some reason that nobody knows, Melinda went into Philadelphia, several hours after I had left for Allentown. She could have had an unspoken appointment or been looking for something to add to the apartment, no one will ever know for sure. Tragically, she had been critically injured in a multiple car accident on the Schuylkill Expressway. Emergency crews had to cut from her car and she was air lifted to Philadelphia Mass General where she was listed in critical condition and placed on life support. Her doctors labored around the clock and did everything possible to keep her alive.

Unfortunately, Melinda's injuries were catastrophic and to everyone's great horror she never regained consciousness. She passed away early Wednesday morning with her family gathered around her. I was the only person in her world that did not know she was dead. Wednesday evening I tried calling from Allentown but I got no answer at either the apartment or at her mother's house.

This seemed unusual, however my shoot was busy. Every day I had a line of mothers wanting to have their babies and young children photographed so my week went by fast. Still, no matter when I called, I couldn't get an answer at either the apartment or the house. By Friday I knew that something had to be wrong. My inability to get in contact with Melinda was now a source of great anxiety. I finished my photo shoot late Saturday evening, packed up my gear and headed straight to Brooklawn.

I had to know what was going on and I prayed that not being able to communicate with her was just a matter of bad timing. She lived a busy life and I didn't expect her to sit by the phone waiting on me to call. But that was just it. She would wait by the phone for me to call and I had always been able to get in touch with her when I was out of town. I arrived at the apartment around 10 PM but Melinda wasn't there so I called her mother's home. This time I got a busy signal. Now I knew something was wrong.

So I got back into my car and drove to her house. Along the way various scenarios flooded my brain but my first thought was that something must have happened to her mother or brother. I never for a second thought that something might be wrong with Melinda. She was permanent, angelic, guarded by heavens own good graces. No way could anything be wrong with her.

When I got there I was surprised by the number of cars in the neighborhood. Her Mom's front yard was full of cars and both sides of the road were lined. So I circled the block and parked down the street, as close as I could get. When I got to the house I found the front door open and I thought this to be a little odd. I entered the house and immediately found myself in a sea of well dressed strangers.

It looked like everyone had just been to church and I found this a little unsettling. Slowly I worked my way through this crowd of strangers until I found Melinda's brother. When he saw me he grabbed me by the arm and guided me to Melinda's mother and together the three of us walked out to the backyard.

Chapter 39

We sat down at a table on the deck and slowly Melinda's mother told me everything that had happened. They didn't leave anything out. The car wreck had occurred Tuesday morning and Melinda had died of her injuries Wednesday morning. Her funeral had been held Saturday morning and she had been buried around two o'clock that afternoon. I was devastated. It felt like the weight of the world had suddenly fell on me. This was impossible.

It had to be a mistake. This was the girl of my dreams. I couldn't get my mind around the fact that she was actually gone. We were going to spend our lives together. But now none of that would ever happen. My one and only, most beautiful angel in the world was dead. Our relationship had died with her. I was completely and utterly alone. I was shocked to the core and as my life was soon to express, that shock would be carried, in my heart, for decades.

I asked to see her grave and her brother agreed to take me there. We drove to the church and her brother led me to her grave; a freshly back filled mound covered with green outdoor carpet. I couldn't get past the fact that she was dead. She had become the biggest, brightest, most spiritual part of my life and now the place in my heart that she had occupied was vacate. It was bloody and dead, like an abortion. In her place a ravishing monster appeared, ready to inflict endless grief and gut wrenching torment.

I told her brother that he could go home. I wanted to stay and he had said that I could stop by the house if I needed anything. But he didn't have what I needed. In one horrifying hour I had been plunged into a nightmare from which there was no escape. I prayed for Melinda to step from the shadows and make the pain that twisted my guts go away. But, she didn't and the longer I sat there, trying to wrap my mind around the obvious, the more I had to face the fact that she was never coming back. For the first time in my life I had been in love with a woman who brought out the best in me and now she was gone.

I had never thought about it in these terms but life is fragile at best. Love is precious, cherish your lover because losing them is beyond terrorizing. It is crushing and nightmarish. It is worse then organ failure. It tears a hole in you. A hole that will not heal. Its hard to live with such damage and its fair to say that sometimes you never recover. Melinda had been the light in my life and now her light had been snuffed out. I dwelt in total darkness. The grief and sorrow that took her place blinded me. Every person, place or thing that I had once held near and dear to me now paled in comparison to her memory.

Chapter 40

I had bought a fifth of Amaretto and a fifth of vodka on my way into town. Amaretto was Melinda's favorite and I kept it around because she liked it. We drank it every time we were together. So I went to the car, retrieved both and spent the night brooding over her grave. By Sun up I had finished off both fifths and could still feel the pain. It surrounded me, suffocated me, crawled inside of me and took up residence. I thought back over our relationship, from the day we met to the last day I had seen her alive.

I thought about the future we had planned and about the fact that now it would not happen. I felt as empty as the fifth I was holding and to this day I can't smell Amaretto without thinking of her. In fact, there has not been a day since I first met Melinda that I don't think of her. To know who the love of your life is, and to be in this world without them, is torturous.

The vodka had no effect on my mind. Her earthly remains were entombed before me and I was in no hurry to leave. Photographing babies had brought us together and having a baby was something I'm sure Melinda and I would have ultimately done. Now she was gone and I would never go back to that job. With each passing hour my despair increased. I refused to leave her grave.

I had no desire to return to the apartment. It meant nothing to me now. Melinda had made it a home for us. Now it was just a hole in the wall. I was trapped between heart rending grief and a freshly interned grave. Morning came, the Sun rose and I sat frozen in time. I was a stranger in a strange land. Melinda had been my guiding light and now she was gone. I dwelt in total darkness.

I spent the day at her grave drinking. The rug had been

jerked out from under me and now I felt like I was free falling into a deep, empty pit. It was all too much to comprehend and the more I tried the worse I felt. We had only known each other for about six months but that had been enough for us to fall in love and plan a lifetime together. I had left my beautiful, precious angel, healthy, happy and as bright as Sunshine and returned to a freshly dug grave in whose darkness she was now buried.

Did I grieve for my loss and learn ways to cope with my sorrow so that I could move on with my life? No. I was a paralyzed soul and once left to my own devises I came undone. I told my supervisor what had happened, turned in my photography gear and quit my job. He offered me a couple of weeks off, with pay to reconsider, but I was in no mood to make babies smile. I had lost the light of my life. She had been the most precious, loving, spiritual person I had ever known. The realization that she was not coming back slowly sank in and the pain was unreal. In fact, the pain increased with each passing day.

For the next several weeks I drowned my sorrows in vodka. I lived in the graveyard. Slept on Melinda's grave. I was there when her mother visited but there was little to be said. We shared the same grief and when she turned to leave she had invited me to her home for dinner. I couldn't remember the last time I had actually ate something. But I wasn't hungry. My soul was thirsty, not for food – vodka. So I broke open a fresh fifth and drank myself into a stupor. The only time I left her grave was to buy alcohol and cigarettes. Food was the last thing on my mind and there were times when I didn't eat for days.

I told the apartment manager that I was moving out, bought several fifths of vodka and returned to the graveyard. Her mother visited her grave once a week and I was always there. On one such occasion she asked for my mother's telephone number and then again invited me to dinner. This time I accepted her invitation and made plans to join her for dinner the next day. Despite living on nothing but vodka and cigarettes I still felt the pain. I could not drink enough, to get drunk enough, to pass out.

Chapter 41

I had not thought much about giving Melinda's mother my mother's telephone but I had and before I arrived for dinner she had called my mother and told her everything. Beside the sadness of losing her only daughter she was deeply worried about me. I was coming apart at the seams. If somebody didn't intervene on my behalf I would soon be dead. You can't drink as long and as hard as I was drinking and not die. She had arranged a second phone call and after dinner she again called my mother. After a brief conversation she handed me the phone. I talked to my mother for the first time in well over a year.

She had been told everything that had happened over the last six weeks and knew of my current state of mind. I didn't have a job so I didn't have the money to live in New Jersey and she had insisted I return home immediately. I agreed. I could not bring Melinda back. I would never forget her, but I could not sustain my current existence. So I and turned in my keys, said good bye to Melinda's mom, spent my last fifty dollars on gas, a fifth of vodka and two packs of cigarettes. I watched Brooklawn fade in my rear view mirror just as the Sun was setting. I would never go back to New Jersey, would never speak to Melinda's mother and would never quell the raging, pain that Melinda's death brought to my brain.

Between Brooklawn and Danville Virginia I drank that fifth of vodka. It was a twelve hour drive and I had arrived at my parents home around seven the next morning. When I got there I was somewhere between drunk, hungover and exhausted. I took a shower, fell into bed and slept for two days. When I finally woke up I wandered, lost in thought, into the kitchen, and sat down at the table.

I barely noticed that my mom had joined me. She took my hand and asked if there was anything more to Melinda's death than what her mother had told her. I didn't know what Melinda's mother had said so I told her everything. For me it was an unimaginable tragedy. Melinda had been critically injured in a car accident. The doctors had done all they could but she died the next day and had been buried before I even knew she was dead.

To say that I wasn't handling it very well was an understatement. Coming back to find her dead was a nightmare I couldn't wake up from. Melinda was my first true love. We were planning to get married and spend a lifetime together. I couldn't image anyone ever taking her place. My mom had been very sympathetic. She had lived through the death of her oldest son and she didn't want anything happening to me. Unexpected death was tragic, no question about it.

But she also reiterated the belief that I had to get on with my life. I was young and time would heal my wounds. The pain would fade. But I had to be careful. Grief was a weight so great it could crush you if you let it. You had to get out from under it or it would kill you. There was nothing wrong remembering Melinda. I could keep what she meant to me safely in my heart. It was unreasonable to think I would forget her. However life was for living and I needed to get on with mine.

Chapter 42

It would take many years to recover from the gnawing grief that savaged my guts because of Melinda's death. Truthfully, I don't think I ever did. Even now, thirty-five years later, I still think about it. To dull the pain of her loss I drank heavily. I lost my interest in photography and took a job selling flooring for a store named ColorTile. This job was in Winston-Salem. It required a lot of heavy lifting which was exactly what I needed.

I worked nine hours a day. There were trucks to unload and customers to satisfy. As it turns out I was well suited for this type of work. After six months I was promoted to assistant manager and six months later I was promoted to store manager. I promoted the store's top salesman to assistant manager and hired a salesman to take his place. The store was open six days a week, Monday through Saturday, twelve hours a day, from 8 AM to 8 PM. Managers worked from 11AM to closing and had Friday and Sunday off while assistant managers opened the store at 8 AM, worked to 5PM and had Sunday and Monday off. My two salesmen worked a rotating schedule that had them off Sunday and one week day.

On the surface it appeared that I was recovering from my grief but in truth I was just getting better at hiding it. I was self medicating with a steady intake of vodka and pills. I rented an apartment several miles from the store and began to frequent a bar that lay in between. In addition, there was a bar right behind the store and I would often spend my lunch hour there for a couple of beers and a few shots of vodka. For a while my "liquid lunch" got me over the hump. It was the right thing at the right time. A couple of cigarettes and a steady intake of breath mints kept what I did with my lunch hour a secret.

Chapter 43

It seems like my brain has a built in heroin detector that enables it to hone in on smack no matter where I'm at. Maybe my wires are permanently crossed or, as repeatedly demonstrated by junkies everywhere, addiction trumps common sense each and every time. Either way my return to Winston Salem raised the specter of heroin use. I should have been scared to death, but instead I thought about it all the time.

I craved it. Passionately. As if I was in love with it. I knew where to score junk should I elect to do so. I had come a long way since clawing my way back from the brink of heroin based self destruction five years earlier. As I thought about it, the years I spent strung out on heroin and living one step ahead of the law was remembered as being a bit surreal if not romantic.

In truth those years had been terrifying and all to often the people around me died. Truth is most people don't have what it takes to deal with the demons of heroin and death on a regular basis. I knew both of these demons well but I did not consider myself their master. Lives that are based on sex and drugs are generally short-lived. I had just been lucky. Heroin was a world all its own. Trying to marry that world to the work-a-day world of sober people is impossible.

I didn't trust myself with it and I had good reason for not letting it back into my life. So I thought about it from time to time but at this point I was strong enough to resist it and made no attempt to acquire it. I adjusted my poison of choice to conform with my work schedule. As luck would have it I was a good retail manager, had a busy store and no problem making my paperwork reflect positive sales results.

In 1986 I turned twenty-six years old. All that meant was that I had been without Melinda for one year and was two years away from a three year heroin addiction. I wore a mask and put up a good front. I had several drinking buddies and focused on three things; my job, Melinda and drinking. Occasionally I would catch myself looking for her in the women I met. But I was too damaged to date even when the women went out of their way to let me know they were available.

I ignored them. My life was set in stone. There was no room for anyone new, especially no relationship of a romantic nature. That space in my brain belonged to Melinda and I was not ready to relinquish it to anyone. So I focused on my job and along the way was introduced to a new drug known as Xanax. This drug was far more powerful than Valium and greatly helped me with my sleep.

Chapter 44

Then came someone that flew in the face of my romantic moratorium. One morning I was sitting at the store's main counter trying to recuperate from late nights drinking when a beautiful woman came in. She handed me a business card, introduced herself as Diane and told me that she was a professional wallpaper hanger. She was there to see if the store could refer her for some installation jobs.

Through my normal morning fog I noticed several things at once. First was her hair. She wore her hair in the exact same style that Melinda had worn hers. Second was her stature. She was petite. Five foot, four maybe five inches tall, and no more than one-hundred and twenty pounds. Just like Melinda.

The third thing I noticed was her confidence, which manifest itself in the way she carried herself. She had definitely graduated from some college somewhere so self employed wallpaper hanger seemed a little odd, but to each his own. I was in no position to question anybody's choices about anything. Her story was probably interesting and I liked the way she exhibited an air of personal strength.

She had the ability to go after and get anything she wanted and I liked that. For the first time in almost two years a woman other than Melinda had entered my mind and I was surprised to realize that I was attracted to her. This was interesting and unsettling at the same time because I had built a massive wall around myself and I was pretty content with its construction.

Sure it was built of vodka, Xanax, pain and fear, but up to now it had done the trick. No woman had ever gotten through and I don't know how, but somehow Diane had managed to slip past my defenses. The whole purpose for building the wall was to preserve Melinda's memory. Diane was distracting and I was amazed by how quickly she got my attention. I walked her over to my wallpaper department and said that we had people asking for installers so I knew I could steer business her way. She handed me some business cards to give interested customers and turned to leave. But I was not ready to let her go. Her similarities to Melinda were startling. They could have been twins. So I asked her what size jobs was she looking for and she had said she could handle just about anything.

Chapter 45

I wanted to know more about her. I had never met anyone who so closely resembled Melinda. When I felt the time was right I asked her in what month of the year she was born. Diane had smiled brightly and said "August the 21st, 1962." I was floored. Melinda had been born on August the 12th 1962. There were so many similarities between the two and I had more questions than answers. She had definitely peaked my interest. But this was business not pleasure and while she was definitely interesting it was not enough to get me to step out of my comfort zone.

So I said good bye, attached her business cards to the bulletin board and went back to work. In fact, over the next few days she slipped from my mind and she did not return until a local contractor came in looking for a wallpaper hanger. I remembered Diane and had pointed out her business card. I offered to let him use the store's telephone and he called her immediately. They talked for a while and set up an appointment to met at the job site and work out a deal.

As it turns out the job was a very large apartment complex. Sixty-five units, each requiring one kitchen wall, a bathroom and a foyer. It was a large job for one person but Diane needed the work and accepted it. She stopped by the store to thank me and while talking about it she expressed her concern about by the size of the job. This was the largest thing she had ever done and I was surprised to hear myself offer to help her on Fridays. It was like my mind had become disconnected from my mouth.

My brain was screaming "no" but my tongue was saying "yes, I'd be happy to help you."

To my surprise she accepted my help and we planned

for me to start that coming Friday. I suddenly wished I hadn't made that offer. Diane had planted her flag in my brain and now she was inside my head. She was cutting into my drinking time and I did not like that one bit. But I had made the offer and I was not going to back out now. Was I getting her mixed up with my memory of Melinda? Was I comparing the two in my brain and Diane was coming out on top simply because she was alive?

As it turned out Diane was not a slave driver and I had no intention of working hard. I was there to help and to observe the process. Truth was I spent all my time mourning Melinda's death and had came to the conclusion that no one could ever take her place. I wasn't sure I even wanted someone to take her place. Then, as if by magic, there was Diane and while I knew nothing about her, she had peaked my interest. I helped her every Friday and each day I got to know her better.

Initially I didn't think I had much to offer, but the work was doable and I learned a lot from Diane. We worked well together and on the days I helped her we knocked off nine units, which put her ahead of schedule. After just three weeks Diane was almost done and felt sure that one more week would finish the job. The contractor was happy and I was glad to be nearing the completion of my obligation.

Along the way Diane and I had became good friends. She was a patient listener. We talked a lot about our past and the events that had brought us to this particular crossroads. Diane tore down a lot of my wall by listening to the parts of my story I was willing to share. She had also experienced life changing losses and the more we talked the more we liked each other. We shared many experiences, no question about it, but we were two entirely different people. I was a recovering heroin addict and a burgeoning alcoholic. She was neither. I didn't talk about my demons and Melinda was completely off the table.

Chapter 46

We finished the job two weeks ahead of schedule and Diane was very happy to see that contractor write her a check. With my help she had made good money in a relatively short period of time and she had offered to pay me for my time. But I said "No." I had learned a new craft and that would help me train my employees to more effectively sell wallpaper. For me that was a big deal and I had suggested we go out to dinner the following weekend to celebrate our success.

Diane had eyed me curiously, handed me one of her business cards and said; "Okay, call me with the details and we'll do it." At this point there was no rush, or at least I didn't feel rushed. Our knowledge of each other was more business than pleasure and the suggestion of a dinner date didn't change that. I had not been able to drink a lot during the time I helped Diane so I was parched. I was ready to get drunk and after years of heavy drinking I was a powerful drinker. I could drink everyone I knew under the table and still drive home. I had never thought about what this might look like to a non-drinker.

With the wallpaper job over I turned my attention back to vodka. By midnight Saturday I was drunk and with the aid of several Xanax had enjoyed a good night sleep. I laid around Sunday so that I would have a clear head Monday. The week proved busy with a large truck on Tuesday and a major restocking that took until Wednesday afternoon to complete. By Thursday the store was and in perfect order. Sells were good so I cut the books early, sent my salesmen home and closed the store alone.

Friday was my first off day of the week and I had called Diane a little after lunch. She sounded happy to hear from me and after exchanging pleasantries I asked her to join me for dinner Sunday evening. If that had not worked I probably would have never called her again but she said "okay" and I chose my favorite restaurant as our meeting place. We agreed on 6 PM and I told her to look for me at the bar.

Chapter 47

Sunday came soon enough and I arrived at the restaurant a couple hours early for the express purpose of catching a good buzz. By 6 PM I was on my way to drunk and Diane had arrived as planned. After a short wait we got a table and ordered drinks as well as an appetizer to get the afternoon started. We had the advantage of knowing each other so our conversation began with questions like what kind of week I had to what kind of jobs she was working on. She was suddenly very busy and happy to have so much work. It was mostly bathrooms and kitchens but it would keep her busy for the next few weeks.

By the time our entrees were served I had downed four more beers and was feeling no pain. She waited as I ordered my next beer and then said; "I'll tell you something you don't know about me. Before my wallpaper business, I was a police officer. Cops are trained to look for certain things and I can see that your catching a pretty good buzz. How are you going to get home?"

I had never gave this much thought. I drove drunk all the time. So I said; "I don't know. I have friends at the bar, maybe I'll call a cab or maybe I'll drive."

"Tell you what. Drink all you want and I'll make sure you get home in one piece. I just don't want you driving drunk." I thought about it for a second and said, "Okay, whatever you think. But you don't have to worry about me. I always manage to get home." That was true, but I did drive drunk a lot and I knew I was taking a chance. But then my whole life, up to this point, had been based on risky behavior. My response seemed to please her because she had said; "Perfect. Now you can drink all you want. I don't mind. When you're ready I'll get you home."

I don't know why I felt the need to explain my drinking but for some reason I did and had told Diane that I suffered from chronic insomnia. I had a lot on my mind. There were skeletons in my closet and my past was haunted. Most of my friends were dead and I needed large amounts of alcohol and Xanax to get any sleep. Even then my nights were restless and sometimes I didn't sleep for days.

Diane had said that the smartest thing to do would be visit a doctor. Explain my situation and get help treating my insomnia. She went on to say that she suffered from insomnia but her doctor had prescribed her a pill and she took it daily to make sure she slept every night, without incident or side effect. I had never thought about going to a doctor and had absentmindedly said; "interesting."

I had connections. I didn't need a doctor.

Chapter 48

S

uddenly I felt exposed. Diane was trying to get inside my head and I had said too much. I had endured problems sleeping since I was twelve years old. At this point my biggest fear was that Diane would try to trace my insomnia back to its source. I needed to change the subject so I said; "I'm going to get one more beer and then we can get out of here." Diane sensed my discomfort and moved quickly to calm me down by saying; "don't worry. We're in no hurry."

So I drank two more beers, paid the bill and before leaving stopped by the bar to introduce Diane to my buddies. I ordered another beer and we spent the next fifteen minutes talking to a bunch of very drunk people. But we weren't staying and once outside Diane had guided me toward her car. "Don't worry" she said, "I'll get you back in time for work. Make sure your car's locked. I'm sure it will be fine."

She was being polite but firm and I had went along because it was easier than not. However, I was out of my comfort zone and I found myself thinking about Melinda. It felt like I was betraying her. Now all I could think about was the wall. My only choice was to go with the flow. A couple beers and a couple Xanax would put me to sleep and morning would come soon enough.

We arrived at my apartment within fifteen minutes and I had remarked about how close the restaurant was to my home. "Yes" Diane said; "but if you had drove you would have been driving drunk and I just couldn't let you do that." I thought about that and then said to her. "Diane, if you're planning on being my new angel there's a few things you should know. I have devil's in my backyard and skeletons in my closet. My past is haunted and my brain is fried. I disappoint, that's what I do.

And I can't be regular. Just beneath the skin I'm fifty shades of dysfunctional. You could do better than me without trying."

We came to my apartment and I opened the door for her. I stepped to the side to let her enter, but she was looking at the door. "You don't keep your door locked? Aren't you afraid you might get robbed?" I motioned for her to enter and followed her inside. I turned on the kitchen light, opened the freezer and got a handful of Xanax from their bottle.

I opened the refrigerator for a beer and swallowed the pills as Diane looked around. As she went she turned on the lights and as she did the apartment came to life. "You know Steve, you're not the only one living with regrets. I have a few myself. Everybody does. That's life. You learn from it and move on. You've got to leave the past behind. If you don't, you will stuck looking backward. Sometimes you're better to let life carry you along."

I joined her on the couch and said; "Sounds good in theory but in some cases it's easier said than done. In fact I would dare say that life drags you along whether you like it or not. There are times when it actually picks you up and throws you against the wall or scrambles your world like it was a couple of eggs. In fact the more you try to hang on to the less there is to hang on to. Sometimes I feel like I'm just waiting for the next shoe to drop."

"Is that why you drink so much?"

I yawned. The Xanax and beer were beginning to work their magic. I was going to sleep and nothing would stop me. "I don't know... I've been drinking since I was sixteen." I kicked my shoes off and put my feet up on the coffee table. "That's ten, going on eleven years." I yawned again. "I guess that's a long time in some people's book... I guess it is. I know a lot of people who have been drinking all their lives. Alcohol helps me relax. Most of the time I'm drinking just to make sure I get some sleep."

Chapter 49

With that I went to sleep or more to the point, I passed out. It was only eleven-thirty, but I was out like a light and that night I slept without dreaming. That was always my goal. No terrifying journey into the darkness, no disembodied voices or insane laughter. No rolling around in the bottom of the bowl. Just the sweet relief of sleep guaranteed by near lethal combinations of drugs and alcohol. I woke up around 6 AM and saw that I was sleeping on one end of the couch with Diane curled up on the other end. I got up, started the coffee maker and took a shower.

I was stiff from sleeping on the couch and dealing with a heavy mental fog from the beer and Xanax. But I had six hours to sober up. So I got dressed and went down stairs to find that Diane was awake.

"Good morning Sunshine, how about a cup of coffee?"

"Sounds great, got any milk?"

"No milk, just creamer."

"Okay, I'll take a little creamer. Do you always get up so early?"

I handed her a coffee cup and the creamer and said; "It all depends on how early I go to bed. Sleeping on the couch didn't help. I'm hungover and hungry so while I don't have to go in until lunch I do need to eat something and maybe take a quick nap. Let's see what the weather's going to do today."

We spent a few minutes watching T.V., and then Diane asked if she could take a shower. I said; "Sure. Towels are in the upstairs bathroom, help yourself." I watched her disappear up the stairs and found myself admitting that I didn't mind having her around. I had spent a lot of time with her lately and it was nice not being alone. I was comfortable being by myself but I did spend a lot of time passed out.

Chapter 50

Diane returned to the living room after her shower and sat on the edge of the couch drying her hair. She ran her fingers through it and shook her head to give it volume. She could be sexy without trying and I had to wonder if she knew the effect she was beginning to have on me. When she finally came out from under the towel I said; "When you're ready we'll go get some breakfast."

"That sounds great. I'm ready now."

I sat my coffee cup in the sink and Diane followed suit. However she stayed long enough to rinse both cups, then checked the coffee maker to make sure it was off. We walked out the front door, which she made sure was locked. She was being caring for me in the simplest of ways. It seemed like she wanted our relationship to be more than it currently was. I couldn't see her getting much closer than she was.

We ordered our food and found a table where we settled in to eat. We busied ourselves with wrappers and spoons and were relatively quiet for a while. I was wondering how she felt about last night when she said; "I hope you didn't get the wrong impression last night. I wasn't prying. I was just concerned. You're a nice guy. I'd like to get to know you better. I don't want anything bad happening to you."

"No need to worry. Like I said if I had actually needed a ride someone would have gave me one."

We finished our meal and left McDonalds for the fifteen minute drive back to the restaurant we had eaten at the night before. As I opened the car door I said; "Come by the store later this week and I'll give you a list of contractors who have wallpaper needs."

"Okay, I will. I had a good time last night and I'd like to do it again."

"Sure, we'll talk."

We met in the middle for our first kiss, after which I got out of her car, into mine and waited for her to leave. Once she was gone I returned to the apartment, set my alarm for 11:45AM and went back to sleep. I woke up two hours later feeling better and after taking a couple Xanax had went into work. My salesman punched in with me and that let my assistant manager and his salesman go to lunch.

Chapter 51

That's the way it went. The store was in good shape but working stock kept us busy and was something we did all the time. Cull small lot patterns and move them to a discounted area I had at the front of the store. People were always looking through this area hoping to do their jobs cheap. This enabled me to order large amounts of specific patterns with the same lot number. 4 PM came and to help my jitters I walked to the bar behind the store for a couple of beers and several shoots of vodka.

That did the trick and by 6 PM we were down to a few browsers so I sent everybody home and cut the books. I was ready for a good night sleep so when I got home I took a round of Xanax, opened a beer and settled on the couch. After watching a little T.V., I took a shower, drank several shots of vodka, took a couple more Xanax and went to bed.

I went to sleep almost immediately and slept late the following morning. I showered, dressed, ate lunch and arrived at the store around noon. At 5 PM the day shift left and at 6 PM I let my salesman leave to save on hours. It was almost time to close when Diane came through the front door and walked up to the counter. She was smiling and I smiled back asking, "How are you?"

"I'm fine. I came to see if you have that list of contractors you promised me."

"I do. In fact you caught me at a good time. I don't have anything to do. Let me get my files. While I do take a look at the bulletin board. Introduce yourself to other wallpaper hangers. A lot of times they need help. Put a few of your cards up there and be prepared to put more. Customers are always taking them."

So while Diane looked over the bulletin board I retrieved my contractor files and sat back down on my stool. I watched her write down a few telephone numbers and attach several of her cards. She got cuter every time I looked at her and I had seen her enough now to start noticing how sexy she was. But this was a distraction so I focused on my files and selected twenty leads. "Call these people and introduce your business. Set up meetings and talk to them face to face. When you call apartments and hotels tell them you also repair damaged paper. Keep a photo album of your work. Hand out business cards and establish a call back schedule. Never let them forget you."

"Okay. That sounds like good advice. When's your next day off?"

"Friday and Sunday. I'm always off Friday and Sunday."

"Let's get together and do dinner, or lunch. Your choice."

"Okay. Not Friday. Check with me Saturday. Maybe we can do lunch Sunday."

"Perfect. Tell you what, this time, since I'm asking you out, I'll pay and that will make us even."

"We'll see. Just call me Saturday to make sure I feel like it. Sometimes all I do on Sunday is lay around. Maybe we could lay around together. You know; grill out, watch a couple of movies."

"Sounds perfect. I'll call you Saturday afternoon."

Chapter 52

    With that Diane left and at 8 PM I closed the store and drove to the bar where I drank a few beers, had a shot of vodka and talked to my Xanax connection. Once home I grabbed a handful of Xanax, drank a couple shots of vodka as well as a few more beers. I went to bed thinking I would have a good night but I didn't sleep well. I had a new dream. In this one a man came into view as a dot on the horizon and walked toward me growing larger as he came. When he got close I could tell that he was covered in a layer of ashes and dirt. He was gray, seemingly lifeless, but his eyes were two pools of blood. As he came closer he faded, growing thinner and thinner, until finally he stood before me as thin as a late morning fog. He opened his mouth to speak and fell into a pile of dust at my feet.

    I also dreamed of Diane. In my dream she appeared to be dead. I couldn't make out how or why. She just lay there in a pool of blood. Her eyes were blue – lifeless blue; the same color as my Xanax. These dreams were disturbing and they woke me up. I thought about them for a good hour and couldn't go back to sleep. So around 3AM, I got out of bed long enough to take several Xanax and drink a beer. But it didn't help. I was restless and I tossed and turned until finally I gave up and got up.

    I spent Friday recovering from a horrible night. I wasted the entire day and took every Xanax I had to insure I got a descent night sleep. Saturday morning came around and while I hadn't dreamed the night before I was preoccupied by my latest dreams. I was amazed I could remember them with such detail and I was happy to lose myself in a little hard work.

    I turned my attention to the heaviest materials and spent three hours merchandising the marble and ceramic floor tile sections. I then spent another two hours merchandising the setting materials and at four-thirty I let my assistant manager and his salesman leave for the day. I kept busy sweeping the store and around 6 PM, my Xanax connection came in. It was a simple monthly arrangement; three-hundred pills for three hundred dollars.

At this point I was very much in control of my drugs. Or, so I thought. From where I stood I had found a drug that when mixed with the right amount of alcohol effectively knocked me out. I took ten a day, always at night, along with vodka, and this guaranteed a good night's sleep. So I didn't view this as an illegal drug transaction. I was buying what I needed and while some may have viewed it as dangerous but I did what I had to for my personal situation.

Chapter 53

My weekend didn't go as planned. Thursday night had been filled with new nightmares and Friday had been a restless day followed by a restless night. These new dreams were forcing me to reformulate my medicinal requirements. The whole week had now been messed up by bad sleep and nightmares. Diane was on my mind a lot and so by Thursday I had decided to avoid her this coming weekend. I spent a few hours Friday visiting my parents and on Saturday morning I told my staff to answer all calls and tell anyone who called for me that I had gone to meet a contractor. They could take a message but were told to not promise a call back until sometime next week.

True to her word Diane had tried to get in touch with me several times on Saturday, but my employees did as they had been instructed and I closed out the day without talking to her. After closing the store I stopped by the bar to have a few beers and then went home where I eat twenty Xanax and continued drinking until 2AM. I went to bed so drunk that I didn't wake up until I felt myself being shaken and in the distance heard someone saying my name.

"Steve, Steve, wake up wake up... Come on wake up... It's after lunch."

I opened my bloodshot eyes and through the haze saw Diane sitting on the edge of my bed.

"Where did you come from?" I asked sleepily.

"Well when I couldn't get in touch with you yesterday I decided to ride over here to see if you were all right. Your front door was unlocked so here I am."

My first attempt to get up did not go well so I gave

Diane my wallet and sent her after some food. But I didn't get up. I was suffering from a near fatal overdose and simply passed back out. Several hours later and Diane again shook me awake. "I'm back. If you'll get up and eat you'll feel better."

She watched me struggle to pull on my sweats, helped me wobble down the stairs and kept me from strangling when I went back to sleep with food in my mouth. I'm quite sure if she knew what she was looking at she would have called 911. I gave up on food, stretched out on the couch and promptly went back to sleep. When I woke up again it was a after midnight and I didn't see Diane so I assumed she had gone home. I took a handful of Xanax, brushed my teeth and headed for bed.

Chapter 54

That's when I found Diane. She had not left when I went back to sleep, but had spent the day watching T.V., and after taking a shower had slipped into a camisole and went to sleep in my bed. When I found her there I was pleasantly surprised. She was stunningly beautiful and almost naked. Long legs and tiny panties, curves defined by satin and lace. I watched her breathing slow and peaceful. She knew where she was and she wasn't afraid so I climbed in beside her and promptly went to sleep. Around 6 AM, she propped herself up on one elbow and shook me awake with an enthusiastic; "Surprise!"

I looked at her through my usual morning fog and said; "Yeah. You are most definitely a surprise. I didn't realize how beautiful you are until I found you in my bed."

She rolled over, draped her leg across my waist, leaned in for a long slow kiss and then looked me in the eye. I ran my fingers through her hair, looked into her beautiful blue eyes and kissed her softly. I teased her lips with my tongue and then slipped past them. Her tongue pushed back and I pulled her to me, gently sucking her bottom lip into my mouth. This brought Diane to life. She was a mixture of lady and lace, innocence and pheromones, satin and raw sexuality.

She rolled over and straddled me, looked deeply into my eyes as if searching for a hint of what to do next and then lay down on my chest. My hands gently encircled her waist and I ran my fingers down the inside her thighs. She pulled her knees to my waist, nuzzling my neck and purring as I stroked her upturn-ed bottom. She squirmed in delight as I gently probed with my fingers, pushing her panties in and out and then pulling her camisole from her waist to her neck.

Diane sat up, pulled it over her head and tossed it aside. She then lowered herself onto me. She was the perfect vision of wanton sexual beauty. She spread her legs until she was satisfied with her position while I placed my hands on her waist and pulled her back and forth. She lay down on me, heart beating on my chest, her breath hot on my neck and quietly moaned her approval. Then she straightened up, arched her back and pressed down hard will I rocked her back and forth, slower and slower, harder and harder until she erupted in orgasm.

She was pleasantly exhausted, however I was far from finished with her. I rolled her over, crouched above her and kissed her mouth, her neck, her ears, and her breasts. Her stomach quivered as I kissed my way to her belly button, slowly and deliberately, each new kiss calling forth a moan or a whimper. I removed her panties, slowly kissing the skin just below her belly button. My tongue traced her lips and kissed her thighs as I slid her panties down her legs. She lay before me naked and free.

She hummed softly, tossing her head from side to side, as I spread her legs and used my hands to lift her into a position that would let me trace her lips with my tongue, down one side and up the other. I pulled her clit from its hiding place, sucking it in and out of my mouth. I used my fingers to push its delicate hood out of the way. Diane rolled her hips as I made love to her with my lips. I sucked her into my mouth, released her and sucked her in again. Her stomach muscles quaked as she breathed deeply, relaxing into the pleasure. I continued my leisurely pace, keeping her on the edge of orgasm, but never letting her cum. She moaned quietly, breathed deeply and ran her fingers across her stomach.

Every fiber of her being was focused on my mouth. I sucked her in and out, gently holding her with my lips and then slowly applying pressure, sucking harder, then releasing. I pulled her in and out until she moaned "oh god, I can't take this anymore." I ran my tongue between her lips and returned to her clit. She whimpered and ran her fingers through my hair begging for release. I sucked her into my mouth, slowly let go, then sucked her in again. She was now beyond herself and thrashed her head from side to side. "It's not fair" she moaned, "you know I'm ready. You're just being mean."

She wrapped her legs around my neck, pulled me to her and held me there. I sucked her in and out of my mouth, tracing her lips and lashing her with my tongue. Within seconds Diane was breathing fast and shallow as she focused on my tongue. She held my mouth tightly with her legs and exploded in orgasmic rapture. "Oh god... oh god...oh god." I kept sucking her in and out of my mouth, pushing my tongue in and out of her until her orgasm rolled from one into two into an endless orgasmic wave.

I continued sucking her into my mouth until she moaned in protest and pushed me away. I licked her lips then kissed her thighs, her stomach, her breasts and finally her mouth. She looked me in the eye, wrapped her arms around my neck and said "Wow. That is not what I expected when I crawled into your bed." We lay there together in satisfied relaxation and drifted into a light sleep. After an hour or so I woke her up with a kiss and whispered; "let's take a shower. It's still early."

That morning Diane and I became sometime greater than the sum of our parts. We became lovers and Diane took Melinda's place in my life. The wall was being torn down and Melinda was relegated to the realm of distant memory. It was a reality I had once thought impossible. But there she was and for that brief moment in time there was absolutely nothing I would do to change our relationship.

We had both suffered through our share of broken dreams but for now, right there, in that moment, we fell in love without saying a word. But then sex doesn't mean love and it would probably be more accurate to say that the only missing component was a love we know we could trust. The love we knew wouldn't break. We were preparing ourselves for that but there were still a lot of un-answered questions and a lot of things had been left unsaid. All of this would eventually be addressed, but for that morning the world fell away and it was just us.

There's another world inside of me that you may never see
There are secrets in this life that I can't hide
Somewhere in this darkness there's a light that I can't find
Maybe it's too far away, or maybe I'm just blind...

Maybe I'm just blind

So hold me when I'm here, right me when I'm wrong.
Hold me when I'm scared, and love me when I'm gone.
Everything I am and everything in me
Wants to be the one you wanted me to be.

I'll never let you down even if I could
I'd give up everything if only for your good.
So hold me when I'm here, right me when I'm wrong
Hold me when I'm scared... You won't always be there

So love me when I'm gone.

When your education X-Ray cannot see under my skin
I won't tell you a damn thing that I could not tell my
friends.
Roaming through this darkness, I'm alive but I'm alone
Part of me is fighting this, but part of me is gone.

Maybe I'm just blind...

Three Doors Down: Away From The Sun: When I'm Gone
Bradley Arnold, Matthew Harrell, Robert Todd,
Christopher Henderson.
Lyrics Published by © Universal Music Publishing Group. 2002

Chapter 55

A wise man once said that you could have anything you want in this life. Just be prepared to give up everything else for it. So before you pick your prize you better decide how much you're willing to lose to get it. Is what your willing to lose worth what you stand to gain? Another wise man once said that sometimes you can't get what you want no matter how hard you try. So pick your battles carefully and don't ride into every war that presents itself. Some battles you just can't win. Some battle aren't worth fighting. It is always a good idea to decide whether or not you can stand to lose what you're leaving behind, because while you're away, the mice will play and you may return to a house in ruin.

And then of course the Rolling Stones said it best when they sang; "You can't always get what you want, but sometimes, you just might find, you get what you need." This seems to be the best approach. You don't have to pony up and fight your way through life, or forsake everything for the pleasure of one. In time, life will bring all good things your way and you will get the opportunity to sample its bounty. Patience is key. Prayer doesn't hurt. But you have to realize that if you focus on one thing at the expense of all others you will miss out on everything else life has to offer.

So loosen up. Sample this, avoid that. Be kind, rewind. Take all options into consideration and prepare for change because it will come your way. You must be flexible or you will break. Learn to expect the unexpected because that's usually what happens. In fact, you can almost count on it. You must be quick and nimble. Your ability to duck and weave will determine what you gain, what you lose and how bad a beating you will take along the way. Sometimes doing nothing produces the greatest reward.

I've also learned that somewhere between all and nothing is life's sweet spot. There is a happy medium to be enjoyed. Like the idea of having a glass half full or half empty. This measurement depends largely on your view of life. It has been suggested that the line which determines whether your glass is half full or half empty may very well move up or down depending on your general mental disposition. If you're a positive person life's glass will always look somewhere between half full and overflowing. If you're a negative person life's glass will always look somewhere between half empty and bone dry.

Sometimes I think this glass half full or half empty idea was thought up in a bar by people doing a lot of drinking. Still there is a lot to be said about measuring what life sets before you. This is the safest bet because it implies that you have some control over what you consume or how you respond to what life hands you. Sometimes all you need is a taste and sometimes your glass seems bottomless.

Somewhere between positive and negative lies perfection. Calm, happy, satisfied. Yet we seldom enjoy this perfectly balanced state of life because we're to busy racing back and forth between the extremes. Its hard to sit still and enjoy the harmony. It's hard to happily sample what life serves up today without regretting yesterday or freaking out over what might be on tomorrow's menu. All to often this is the way we live our lives. We're human and sometimes we get our wires crossed. We revert to our instincts and that results in a messy life. It's fight or flight and substance abuse just makes it worse. Like John Cougar said; "I know there's a balance, I see it when I swing past."

Chapter 56

I left for work about a quarter to noon and Diane stayed in bed for several more hours. She woke up pleasurably exhausted, if not a little sore. She took another shower, made the bed perfectly, placed her camisole on my pillow and went downstairs for a cup of coffee. She then left the apartment, locking the front door as she went and I didn't see her again until Wednesday afternoon when she came by the store looking for leads and wanting to know why I didn't woke her up when I left for work.

"Because you were sleeping. I didn't want to disturb you. You look good sleeping in my bed."

She smiled and said; "I slept until way past lunch. I felt incredible and didn't get anything done all day. I don't think I've ever felt that good. You wore me out. I've never cum so many times."

"Are you humming?"

"More like buzzing. Monday morning was incredible. We went someplace new. I feel safe around you now. Our relationship means more than it did before. Being with you feels natural. I love where we seem to be heading. I want to build something with you that has meaning – that will last. Maybe lead from dating and sex to falling in love."

"I think I'm jinxed. Bad things happen to people that get close to me. That's my biggest fear and it makes me afraid for you. I've heard that death comes in threes and I'm already dealing with one dead girlfriend. On top of that most of my friends are dead and I keep people at arms length because I'm afraid for them. Are you willing to take that chance?"

Diane screwed up her cute little button nose, drummed

her fingernails on the counter top, looked at the ceiling, then back at me and said; "Yes. We're incredible together and it's not just the sex. We're good together. Although I'll take that kinda' loving every time I can get it. Monday morning was above and beyond anything I could have imagined. I can't wait until we do it again."

"Okay then, how does this coming Sunday sound?"

"That sound's perfect. How was your Monday?"

"We did alright, not great but good. We were busy all day and that's about as good as your gonna get. How about you?"

"One lousy job. I started it yesterday and finished it today. At this rate I'm going to starve to death."

"Not necessarily. When you're not hanging wallpaper work your contacts. When jobs come in schedule them as far in the future as possible and spend your time working your contacts. Play the odds. One in five contacts will become a customer. Thirty contacts a week should get you five or six jobs, maybe more. Working those contacts will pay off as new jobs or lead you to new contacts."

As we were talking a stranger came in and walked up to the counter. I asked if I could help him and he said; "Maybe. I need a wallpaper hanger that can take on a big job and get it done in a relatively short amount of time."

"There you go" I said pointing to her. "This is Diane. My number one wallpaper hanger."

They walked off a spent fifteen minutes talking about the job. Diane had agreed to wallpaper an entire apartment complex. Forty-seven units, in two weeks. That schedule would require that she work seven days a week to finish on time. But she was excited and to help her bring the job in on time she talked to and hired two other wallpapers who agreed to help her a couple of days each week. They all agreed to start the next day. There was no point waiting. She needed this contractor. He had promised her more work. She needed this to feel successful and that would help her confidence.

Chapter 57

The rest of the week flew by and I spent Friday drinking with my friends. I worked Saturday and spent Sunday doing laundry and eating Xanax. I was glad Diane had a big job but I didn't like her working on that side of town on the weekends. I had told her to be careful. She was in a strange neighborhood, in a high crime area, working alone. It wasn't safe. However, she was determined to get that job done so she had elected to work seven days a week. She didn't think working alone was that big a deal.

So while I drank the weekend away Diane hung wallpaper. However, she should have never stayed in that empty apartment complex by herself. By staying there alone she had unwittingly made herself a target. According to Winston Salem Police someone broke into the unit she was working on sometime over the weekend. There were signs of a struggle and she had been murdered; shot twice in the chest at close range. Her clothes were torn, presumably in the struggle, and her purse and car were missing.

When the contractor found her body Monday morning he called the police and they had roped off the area and opened an investigation. The only information they found on her was a Color Tile business card with my name and phone number on it. So they came to the store to make the connection. I told them that I was the store's manager and she was a local wallpaper hanger who came in every now and then looking for work. I had helped her find a couple jobs including the one she was currently doing.

What's the problem?" I asked.

One of the officers had dryly replied, "She's been

murdered. Her body was found by the contractor this morning. It looks like she was shot twice in the chest, at close range, sometime over the weekend. She bled out so we're guessing it happened Saturday night. We couldn't find any of her personal effects so we're assuming she was robbed. Her car is missing and all she had on her was your business card."

I was shocked. Funny thing was I didn't know that much about Diane. We may have been lovers but we were not in love. At this point she was little more than a one night stand. So I looked over the bulletin board until I found her business card and handed it to the officer. "This might help you figure out where she lived, or who she lived with. I didn't know the contractor she was working for. She told me she would have to work seven days a week to get the job done on time and she hired some help but I don't know who she was working with. I handed them a store business card and said; "If you need me you can reach me at this number."

Chapter 58

The next day Diane's murder made the local newspapers front page. The police were very tight lipped. They didn't have any leads they were willing to share with the public, however they did say they were looking for her car, a blue, four-door 1984 Pontiac Sun-bird. No other details were offered, however they had issued a "crime-stoppers" reward of ten-thousand dollars for information leading to the arrest and conviction of the person or persons responsible for her death.

It took a couple of days to fully digest the fact that Diane was dead. In the beginning I had kept her at arms length because of Melinda but she had been making inroads into my life and the morning we made love had changed everything. I never dreamed something like this would happen. In fact before she took that job we had planned to spend Sunday together. What if I had helped her on my day off.

"No...no...no" I screamed in my mind. "I am not responsible for this. Diane was not mine to keep up with." She had not asked for my help and as I thought about it I was glad I hadn't been there. I could not have protected her from a gun wielding assailant. In fact, if I had been there I would probably be dead myself. She should not have stayed on that construction site alone, especially at night. She had failed to take her own protection into consideration and now she was dead. It was horrible and no one could have predicted it, but it was not beyond the realm of possibility, and it could have easily been prevented. All she had to do was leave that job site when everybody else did.

Chapter 59

The next day Diane's car was found at an I-40 rest stop several hundred miles away. It was on fire and by the time the fire trucks arrived very little was left. Certainly nothing to suggest who might be have done this or in which direction they might be traveling. I caught myself thinking a lot about Diane that week. It was the senseless death of someone who had started to become a fixture in my life.

Letting her into my life had been hard and she had put forth quite an effort. Ultimately I was glad she had made the effort and the fact that we had became lovers was just the adult thing to do. So why had she been torn from my embrace just as our relationship turned intimate? Was this the razor's edge of "deserve." Was it a result or a nasty reward? Was it karma and if so whose? Mine or hers?

Diane had reminded me of Melinda in so many ways and I had slowly let her into my life because of these similarities. Now I could add her untimely, violent death to that list. As I looked back over my life I realized that almost every person that had ever gotten close to me had died violently. There were two women on that list and numerous friends. It did make me think. Maybe death was stalking me and picking off everyone that got close. That may sound ridiculous but it doesn't seem that far fetched.

This was all the more reason to rebuild the wall. Not just for myself but to block anyone that might get to close. By walling myself off I was doing everyone a favor. I felt safe inside the wall. My memory of Melinda was behind the wall and now I could add Diane to this monument of dead lovers. I had no idea this would hurt me in the long run or that the worst was yet to come.

Chapter 60

I didn't attend Diane's funeral. I didn't know anyone in her family or circle of friends. Truth was I didn't do funerals. They were just to upsetting. I had went to Ricky's funeral and that had been enough for me. Then there was Melinda's funeral, which I didn't go to because she was buried before I knew she was dead. Her death had driven me into a state of perpetual grief. Diane had skillfully drawn me from my shell. From the way we met, to the friendship we cultivated, from the lovers we became to her shocking death. There were no simple answers. I missed her terribly and my response was predictable.

Just like every other tragedy or unexplained loss and I did what I always did. I held onto it. I obsessed over it. Wrapped myself in it like a blanket and allowed the pain to pull me back into heavy drug use. I didn't party anymore. I approached my life from the angle of a drug addict. I worked, drank and ate pills by the hand full. I ate pills all day long. And then, as if acting on autopilot, I went to a drugstore and bought a ten day supply of syringes. By purchasing those rigs I opened the door to heroin use. I could see the golden eye, waiting on the other side, beckoning me to stumble back into its arms.

I would never forget Diane just like I would never forget Melinda. Instead they became prime examples of what happened to the women I let into my life. My life now drifted between the realities of alcohol, drugs and work. I compartmentalized everything into predictable, repetitive events and lived a plug and play life. Each week had its deadlines and its requirements. Days off were spent drinking and sleeping my way from one pill induced stupor to the next.

Every now and then I would pull my new collection of

rigs from their drawer and study them. Hold them and remember. Memories flooded my brain. I could actually taste smack and deep inside my brain I knew it was just a matter of time before I welcomed that monster back into my life. In fact, as time progressed shooting heroin slowly became an unfulfilled obsession. I knew I had to be careful. This was not a subject you brought up over drinks and I didn't want to tear my arms up shooting pills.

I think I knew that a return to heroin would be the end of me. Maybe not the first shot but smack was a monster that could devour you in a single shot. Maybe I was fine with that. The pain of losing Melinda and Diane was growing by the day and I would never put anyone else in that situation, if not for their sake, for mine. As my desolation grew so did my daring. It was like playing Russian roulette.

Only the most desperate people traveled this road. But I was ready to roll up my sleeves and ride smack straight into oblivion. I remembered the euphoria of my first shot and forgot the hell that every other shot had put me through. Talk about a selective memory. There were no good times. When heroin abuse tears your world apart, you are held prisoner by the smack you buy, by what you could pull into your rig and by what you could successfully get into your veins.

Chapter 61

When thinking about heroin there was a lot of things to consider and I needed help defending myself from heroin creep. So I started a diary in which I listed the pros and cons of being a junkie. This was almost comical. I argued one side and then the other. One minute I was all for it and the next minute I was solidly against it. I scribbled notes about heroin, wrote down song lyrics about heroin and drew pictures of spoons, melting candles, rigs and tombstones with my name on them.

I told you I was sick.

I found myself talking it out. My mind was wrestling with its own devices and if you didn't know what you were looking at you'd think I was crazy. I was becoming desensitized to heroin so maybe I was a little crazy. I was filling the empty spaces with ghosts from my past and for the first time in a long time I began having my decades old nightmare while I was awake.

This hallucination was now challenging my sanity during the day and at night it terrorized my dreams. My heroin journal was just one step along the way to insuring that I would soon reunite with the poison that had nearly destroyed me five years prior. I finally reached the point of no return on Christmas Day. "Merry Christmas." Well that's what people say at Christmas anyway. Except those people have trees to decorate, presents to open, and family and friends to enjoy the day with.

They're not trying to knock themselves out with nerve pills and vodka. But here I was; twenty-six years old and heroin free for four years. Melinda had been dead for about two years and Diane had been dead for about six months. My nights were horrifying as I dreamed my way from one nightmare to the next. One issue had become painfully apparent, I was sick and tired of sober living. There were only two drugs at my disposal; Xanax and vodka and they were getting me nowhere fast. I needed relief I could count on and so on Christmas Day 1987 I decided that heroin would start helping me with my dis-ease.

My mind was made up. I didn't want to be an out of control junkie like I had been my first time around. I just wanted to enjoy a nice smooth heroin high a couple times a week. Just enough to reduce the stress constantly building behind my eyes. For some reason I felt like I deserved this relief. Like I was special or worse, like I had done it once before and could handle it again. Everybody gets high on something. I was no different. My life would all be down hill from here and that would prove most interesting.

Chapter 62

I was amazed by how easy I found my way back to the starting point. Happy Hills was a low income housing project on Winston Salem's south side. It reputation for street level drug dealers was legendary. Some sold weed, others cocaine and still others came with their pockets full of pills. There is a specific language you need to know if you're going to talk to a dealer. One or two words will do. Certainly no pleasantries. Just a simple statement of what you want followed by an approach or a walk away. My first few contacts couldn't help me but my next contact had just what I was looking for.

"What's you want white boy?"

"Hundred dollars worth of heroin."

"You don't look like a junkie to me."

I pulled up my left sleeve and showed him my healthy, track scarred arm.

"Well shit, my mistake. Looks like you know what you're doing. I've seen a lot of arms like that."

He reached into his pocket and pulled out two small tin foil packets. "One hundred dollars."

I handed him five twenties.

"This is my corner. I'm always here."

"Good to know. I'll be back next week."

He threw a third foil packet onto the seat and said; "If I know junkies you'll be back tomorrow. But, here's three. Monday's cut day so I'll see you Tuesday."

Chapter 63

I pulled away from the curb and headed back to my apartment. I was almost giddy with excitement. I had three packets of black tar. For the first time in five years I was in possession of heroin. It was like skydiving without a parachute. There was little chance of surviving the impact, but the flight would be insane and in that insanity you could forget everything. Even if it was only for a few hours at a time.

That was the allure of heroin. Those few hours when smack could push everything out of your mind and you could reside in the billowing, cloud high, white noise that junk provided. Leaving that state of mind was the worst part of sobering up. It was like hitting a wall. You'd etch and shake. Every nerve would burn like fire and only your next fix would make the misery go away. That's the hook. You can't just do one hit and walk away. Your first shot guarantees that you'll be back. Not even the best junkies can leisurely shoot heroin. I knew that. I had spent years in bed with that monster. I knew exactly what I was getting myself into.

Christmas was Friday and the store was closed Saturday and Sunday as part of a three day holiday. This meant I had three days to leisurely reacquaint myself with heroin. I cooked my first hit Friday around lunch and took my time. I kept my loads small and by Saturday night I had finished my first pack and started a second one. I was awash with heroin. A descent amount of smack was always coagulating in my spoon. I could smell it in the air. Feel it in my bones.

It blurred my vision, sent my head into the clouds. But it always brought me back to where I started, and my next shot would repeat the process. The next high would not be as high as the first one. It would not be as fast and it would not last as long. Over the long haul you had to do more and more just to keep up. That's just the way it is. Addiction is repetition. Like a rat on a wheel or a donkey being led around by a carrot.

You have to be careful or you'll overdose and if you go that far you'll probably die. Forget trying to get higher and higher with each shot. The number one rule is not to get higher with each fix but to achieve the same high every time. Sunday was a repeat of Saturday and I cooked the same amount of heroin each time. Just enough to make three one-third of a rig shots with just enough left in the bottom of my spoon to start the next batch.

I had bought enough smack to get through Monday which meant the first thing I had to do Tuesday was go to Happy Hills. When I got there I found my dealer standing on his corner and he laughed when he saw me pull up. Like he owned a well oiled trap and loved watching it spring shut on his victims.

I held up two fingers and he pulled a hand full of tinfoil squares from his pocket and counted them out on the seat beside me. "One, two and three. That's one on the house. How do you like that?"

"You're the man."

He knew what he was doing. Get me hooked on his heroin and I'd be his customer for life. He knew he would make his money back later. The more out of control I became the better he liked it. I would buy more and more of his heroin. It might kill me but I was not a loss he couldn't overcome.

"Be careful with this. It's fresh, so it's powerful. It's hotter then usual. Don't overdose. I need all my customers alive. So enjoy yourself. Just take it nice and slow."

Chapter 64

He spoke like a merchant of death. He saw people like me every day. When it came to his customers he had a photographic memory so when he lost one to jail or death he knew it and he missed them. Heroin addicts hold to a rigid schedule based on how bad their addiction is and how much money they have. I don't think anyone ever satisfies a heroin addiction and he's counting on that. I knew both sides of this equation. When you're dealing drugs your clients are always changing. The only way to be successful is to stand out there on that corner, all day long, avoid the cops and sell to everyone that comes your way.

As I pulled away from his curb a disturbing thought came to mind. How was I going to afford heroin? Xanax and alcohol accounted for all of my disposable cash. I couldn't afford heroin. So I set my mind to saving it. I took a long hard look at my expenses and started by dropping my cable and telephone for a savings of one-hundred a month. I could stop spending so much time in bars and go to the liquor store instead. That saved me another fifty dollars a week and increase my monthly savings to three-hundred.

I stopped buying Xanax which saved me another three-hundred a month and raised my total savings to six-hundred dollars. When my pill connection asked why I told him; "I gotta stop spending so much on alcohol and pills. I'm broke all the time. I'm driving drunk. Fucked up on Xanax. If I keep this up I'm going to kill myself or someone else." He didn't have to know about the choices I made.

The six-hundred dollars I saved allowed me to buy twelve packs of heroin, one pack every three days. If I was careful and exercised a little self control I could make this work.

I also knew that my dealer could get popped at any time leaving me without a connection so I needed to build a stash that would see me through such an inconvenience. Unfortunately for me one square every three days proved to be as thin as I could stretch it. This was the best I could do at this particular point in time and as you might expect my self control did not last long.

Chapter 65

So I picked my poison and let everything else go. Truth was I loved heroin. I didn't like coming down. Jonesing was no picnic and heroin sick was the worst. I didn't like the gut wrenching panic that gripped me when I realized I was out or the mess long term use made of my arms. I didn't mind the time I spent nodding or sleeping but I could do without the way it smacked me awake. Above all I hated the way it lulled me into a false sense of security.

The reality was simple. If I had heroin I was busy doing it. If I was out I was busy buying more. So, I was either taking off like an astronaut or crashing back to earth. The best I could do was one-third of a rig, three times daily with a wash shot at the end of the day to guarantee a good night's sleep. This was my standard and it was meant to be just enough. But, as with everything else, sometimes it was enough and sometimes it wasn't. Some days I felt like I was king of the world and other days, not so much.

And then there was Color Tile; the central cog in my heroin fueled life. In the beginning I had turned my store into a model of retail management perfection. I ran it more by instinct and common sense than anything you could read in a book or pick up at a manager's meeting. My store was ranked number one in sales last year and I was on track to beat those numbers this year. Those numbers put me out in front of every other manager but I was dreading the manager's meeting.

It was scheduled to take place six weeks out, in Charlotte, for a whole week. I knew I could not go in the shape I was in. Showing up nursing a heroin addiction would be the end of my management days. I couldn't think of a single way to miss it. Every excuse that entered my head when I was high got shot down when I was sober. I knew I would only get one chance to excuse myself. I could say that a family member was in the hospital or I could fire my entire staff the week before the meeting and spend the week of the meeting hiring a new one.

But I had a top notch crew. Each of them had been hand picked and trained by me. They worked well together so firing them would be a waste. But then a light went off in my head. If I touted my assistant manager as a "manager in the making" maybe I could convince my Divisional Manager to let him go to the meeting for the benefit of exposing him to other managers. It would be a great opportunity for my Divisional Manager to get a good look at an up and coming store manager.

This idea seemed plausible. It might work. I just had to be convincing. To make it work I had to sell my Divisional Manager on the idea and present it as a rare opportunity or I was screwed. If I went to that meeting I wouldn't make it past day two. I was amazed that my crew hadn't noticed the transformation I was going through. Maybe they noticed and didn't say anything or maybe they didn't know what they were looking at.

Chapter 66

The closer and closer I came to the date of that meeting the more I dreaded making that phone call. But the day came when I couldn't put it off long. I had to know what to do. If I couldn't sell my Divisional Manager on the idea of sending my assistant store manager to the manager's meeting I would need a couple of weeks to wean myself off the junk so that I could go. I might be skinny as a rail, but I would be straight. The day came when I could put the call off no longer.

So I settled myself at my desk, took a deep breath, picked up the phone and dialed his number. When he answered I said; "Hey man... I've got an idea I want to run by you. My assistant manager has been asking me to ask you for a store of his own. I haven't given it much thought but the manager's meeting is coming up and I've got an idea. How about if I send him to the meeting? I know the rules for running a Color Tile hasn't changed in the last year and I think it would be good for you and him."

"How's it going to help me?"

"Well for one you should always be looking for new talent and I believe this guy's got what it takes to be a good manager. He's a good assistant manager and you could broaden his perspective. I also hear that the Greensboro store is failing and since he lives in this area he would make a good replacement. I've taught him everything I can. He can do all the paperwork, place orders, run an inventory. He could take over a store right now. But he needs to get the big picture. That could happen at the meeting."

"I take it you don't want to come?"

"I'm not thinking of me. I've read the 1987 Manager's Handbook from cover to cover. I didn't see any thing new and I think you should always be looking for new managers."

"Alright. I'll let him take your place at the meeting. Give him the store manager's guide and make sure he gets here by nine o'clock Monday morning two weeks from today."

"That's proactive management at its finest. You'll see. He's got what it takes."

"Alright... Send him my way. I'll see just how perceptive you are."

We hung up and I breathed a deep sigh of relief. I had prepared for this minute, no matter the out-come, by bringing a prepared rig to work. I told my help to straighten something and locked myself in the bathroom. I ran hot water over it, working the plunger back and forth, shook it, thumped it and slowly liquefied the heroin inside. I found a vein and fired the whole rig in one long slow motion. It rushed to my head and for a moment I thought I was going to get sick. But that passed and I was soon enjoying the high only heroin could provide. I cleaned my rig, made sure the sink was blood free, slid its cap back in place and put it in my pocket. I washed my face, reentered the store and then went out back to smoke a cigarette. I then went back inside and stared at my store without seeing a thing.

Chapter 67

Here's one thing I know about heroin. It's like Miracle Grow for your character flaws and paranoia was rapidly becoming one of mine. Especially when I was out in public. Was that cop looking at me? Was that woman spying on me? Could I be sowing the seeds of my own demise? I couldn't think of a single thing that my assistant manager could use to stab me in the back. I felt sure that when he heard what I had worked out for him he would be ecstatic. He was getting something he had wanted for a long time.

I had saved myself from exposure and now I could creep back into my opium den. When my assistant came in at twelve o'clock I told put him what I had arranged. He was surprised and excited. I reminded him that this was a rare opportunity and he needed to take full advantage of it. He agreed and I handed him the store's manager guide. I told him to spend the next two weeks memorizing it and be prepared to attend the managers meeting, which started on Monday two weeks from now. It would last a week and all expenses would be paid for by Color Tile. I then excused myself by saying that I had an estimate to do. If I didn't get back in time cut the books around 4 PM and close the store at 8 PM.

"Okay. Thanks, I really appreciate what you've done for me."

"You're welcome. You'll be a store manager before you know it."

Chapter 68

This was an unexpected afternoon off and I spent it resting comfortably in the arms of junk. I sat on the couch, feet on the coffee table and spent the next two hours nodding. As I sobered up my mind drifted back to Diane and Melinda. These were the memories I sought to forget and that ultimately drove my addiction. I wobbled back to the kitchen and poured myself a shot of vodka then fixed myself again. I was good at this. I never lost so much as a speck of junk, not a granule. I had a perfect record and after this hit I was not in any hurry to do more. In fact I felt like this was a good opportunity to exercise a little self control. It was turning out to be an excellent day.

Friday was payday and this one would pay my rent so money would be scarce for the next two weeks. I would have the money to buy four squares and that would give me eight, plus the one I was working on. The paycheck I got two weeks later would be spent on heroin and food. I didn't have much of an appetite but you can't starve to death and I had a list of foods I knew I could eat. Cold cereal with milk, eggs and bacon, soups of almost any kind, apple turnovers, spaghetti, sometimes a hamburger and fries. Nothing else would go down and most everything required a lot of water. But I had a range of foods that would keep me from starving and eating regularly kept me looking somewhat healthy.

Chapter 69

I slept late the following morning and woke up jonesing. I went through the process and after satisfying the demand I got dressed and fixed two additional rigs to get me through the day. I waited until 11AM to shoot the first one and wrapped the other one in a washcloth to carry with me. Customer traffic was slow so I let everyone work until 5 PM and then sent them all home. As soon as they were gone I liquefied the rig I had brought with me and once my comfort level was in place I turned my attention to the stores daily paperwork. I closed at 8 PM and drove straight home.

Once there I spent some time breaking down a fresh chunk of heroin and produced enough liquid tar to make three, one-third rigs, with a left left over. My latest hit had been enough to ease my troubled mind and after an hour or so I decided to try some of the food I had recently bought. That was a lot harder than expected and I had resorted to washing down half a sandwich with several beers. I wrapped up what was left, put in the refrigerator, fixed a large glass of vodka on ice and walked out onto my patio.

Spring was right around the corner and it had been a mild winter. But the air was chilly and after a few cigarettes I was freezing. So I went back inside, donned my bathrobe and sat down on the couch to warm up. Many months had passed since Diane's murder and her death was still a painful memory. I don't know why, but for some reason my mind had returned to her and for the first time since her death I had found myself missing her.

Her death had been senseless, her murder never solved. I couldn't understand why the women in my life died just when it looked like I was going to know the happiness a loving, committed relationship would bring. No point pondering the inequities of love so I liquefied one of the rigs and let the heroin wash over me. I then fixed myself a tall glass of vodka on ice, went upstairs and spent the next few hours drifting in and out of consciousness. Every now and then I took a sip of vodka and slipped back under heroin's veil.

This went on all night. I was jerked awake around 5 AM by a gnawing demand for smack. This was not simply jonesing. This was my body screaming for heroin. The vodka had held me down and allowed my system to run out of heroin. That was not good. Every nerve in my body was on fire. I was shaking and sweating. Hot one minute, cold the next. The lack of heroin twisted my stomach into a knot the size of my fist. All I could do was stumble to the kitchen and fix my next hit.

Chapter 70

I have heard people call dealers "evil people" but he was just satisfying a demand. Maybe junkies were evil. They were the ones who made the demand possible. If it was not for people like me, the dealers wouldn't have anyone to sell to. It was a matter of supply and demand. Dealers and junkies were just different sides of the same coin. I knew this underground economy well. I had spent many years on both sides and now I trying to balance sober living with a raging heroin addiction.

I shot heroin all day long and carried loaded rigs everywhere I went. What could possibly go wrong? I was functioning and nobody was the wiser. I wasn't losing weight or missing work and I was current on all my bills. This brought me back to today. I had rent and my electric bill to pay but I needed enough heroin to last me two weeks so I rode over to Happy Hills looking for a deal.

I had four packs of heroin, plus one that was open, so I wasn't exactly out but I would need at least four more to make it to my next paycheck. I found my dealer, pulled up to the curb and waited for him to get to my truck. "Well, you're either late or early. I see you so much its hard to tell."

"Yeah... I need to work out a deal with you. How about four packs for one-twenty. I got big bills to pay. I'll be broke for the next two weeks. Help me over this hump. I won't make it on the four packs I have."

"Well, I don't do much charity work but you're one of my best customers, so yeah, I'll do that for you."

"Cool... I'm going to have a hard time making it through two weeks on eight packs. Looks like I'll be cutting back just to make it through."

"Hey nobody said this shit was easy. Tell you what. I can

see the monkey on your back. So I'll do you a favor just to keep you coming around. Here's five packs for one-twenty. We'll get back to regular prices the next time you come around. I'll treat you right... But be careful, this stuff is fresh so it's hot..."

"Great man, thanks. I'll be back Friday after next. You can count on it."

That gave me nine packs which meant I had to make each pack last two days. It wouldn't be easy but I could pay my rent and power bill, fill my car with gas and have a little money left over for food. I went straight back to the apartment and added my four new packs to the four I had yet to open. My plan was to spend the afternoon shooting heroin however before starting I set myself to doing laundry. I gathered my dirty sheets, towels and clothes, found six, one dollar bills and went to the complex's laundry where I changed my dollars into quarters and used two washing machines to wash my clothes.

Chapter 71

While my clothes were washing I opened the pack I was working on, drew a little vodka into my rig and carefully rinsed everything down into the bottom of the spoon. I added some water and used my plunger to crush and mix the heroin. I lite my candle and held my spoon over it, stirring constantly to make sure it had all liquefied, then dropped a small piece of cotton into the spoon. I pulled my rig half full, sat the spoon down and thumped the air out. I then slipped the needle into a vein on the top of my left hand. Nothing fancy, no milking blood, just a slow push from my wrist straight to my brain.

Nausea washed over my body and for a minute I thought I was going to vomit. Instead I clinched my teeth and breathed out. I swallowed and breathed. The fog rolled in and for the next two hours I nodded between unconsciousness and the dreamy, fuzzy state of mind brought on by good black tar. After a couple of hours I slowly regained consciousness and began coming out of the deepest part of the hit. Another hour passed before I remembered I had clothes in the washing machine.

So I walked over to the laundry room, moved my wet clothes into two dryers and loaded a couple of quarters into each one. It would take about an hour for my clothes to dry so I opened a beer and stood there trying to get my bearings. My head was buzzing, my stomach churned and for a second it felt like I was going to pass out. But I didn't. I leaned against the counter thinking that a little more in that last hit would have been too much.

I spent the next hour with a beer and a few cigarettes and then I retrieved my clothes. Once back in my apartment I put my clothes away, made up the bed and then went downstairs to clean up the kitchen. Its main counter had been turned into an impromptu prep station with a large plate holding everything I needed to shot dope. I kept at least one pack of heroin in my silverware drawer, along with my rigs, razor blades and spoon. Water was always handy. I kept a stool handy because its hard to ride out a hit standing up and its good to be near the sink in case you get sick. You don't need fancy to get it done.

I thought about my heroin schedule and what I needed it to be. I needed every day to be the same. The same number of hits, the same amount per hit, at the same time every day. My first shot be around 6 AM, my next shot would occur around lunch and my third short would occur around 6 PM. That left me with a rinse shot to do before bed and that always helped me get through the night. The main rule was to standardize my shots and never shoot more than an one-third of a rig at a time.

However, when junk wakes you up it smacks you hard. It's like sleeping with a hand grenade. Jonesing was bad enough but craving heroin so bad that you could taste it was worse. Heroin sick tears you apart from the inside out. Nothing would set you right but your next shot. It would always be your first shot of the day. It could come at 3 AM or sometimes it would hold off until 5 or 6 AM.

Saturday mornings fix hadn't waited for Sunrise. At 2 AM I was jerked awake by my bodies demand for heroin. I no longer tried to rationalize its schedule. When the last hit had run its course I had better be ready or I would be in a world of hurt. When this one hit I was ready and after liquefying a rig I had prepared earlier I satisfied the demand and went back to sleep. I woke up with time to spare and fixed two rigs to carry with me. The day was steady but traffic slowed around 3 PM so once the store was straight I let everybody go home. I fixed myself around 5 PM and finished the day doing paper work.

Chapter 72

The week of the manager's meeting finally came and since my assistant manager was in Charlotte I found myself in the store much more than I liked. I had told my Divisional Manager that I would split the hours between my salesmen and myself. To make that happen without adding hours to my salesmen or saddling them with responsibilities they were not trained to handle I worked a split shift. This meant I opened, worked four hours then left, went home and came back four hours before the store closed.

This worked perfect for several reasons. First I could fix myself before opening and look normal when my morning salesman came in at 8 AM. I could then leave at lunch when my evening salesman came in, let him cover for the morning salesman's lunch hour and when I came back my morning salesman could go home and my evening salesman could go to lunch.

I made this schedule official Monday morning and we worked that way all week. It worked out perfect. Splitting the day into four hour increments meant I never got in a bind because I timed my hits to match my time in the store. Unfortunately things don't always work out the way you would like. On Thursday morning my morning salesman called in to say he was feeling poorly and was going to take a personal day. What could I do? Personal days were a benefit. Each employee had three so I had said okay.

If I had came to the store with a pre-loaded rig or two it wouldn't have been a problem but I hadn't and I wasn't prepared for the long hours. Customer flow was steady so I couldn't leave the store. By the time I left work I was sick.

Driving home was tough. I was jittery, sweating, had a terrible headache. By the time I got home I was shaking so bad I had a hard time fixing my hit. Once my rig was ready I missed my chosen vein, twice.

I tried another vein and missed that one too. My shaking was so bad I finally gave up and just skin popped the whole load. That slowly relieved my pain but it was not the rush I wanted so I prepared another rig and shot it without trouble. But now I had to much heroin in me and this time I did get sick. I made it to the bathroom and puked my guts out. I then gagged for another fifteen minutes. I reached over, turned the shower on and crawled in.

I lay there for two hours unconscious. The freezing water eventually brought me back around and after several failed attempts I managed to crawl out of the tub. I leaned against the wall and took my wet clothes off one article at a time. I found a towel to dry off but I was so high I couldn't put fresh clothes on. So I lay there naked for the next few hours and slowly my buzz relaxed its hold on me.

However it was well after midnight before I could stand up. I had a hard time focusing on getting my clothes on but after a twenty minute fight with a sweatshirt and an innocent pair of 501s I managed to get dressed. This was as close as you could get to overdosing without dying so I felt extremely lucky. Once I got my clothes on I went downstairs to see if the outside world had changed.

It was 3 AM and no one knew what I had been through. I had got about as close to overdosing as you can get without dying. Realizing that was scary however I had survived so now the only thing to do was get some sleep. I would return to my split shift the next day and take a pre-loaded rig with me just in case. This mishap highlighted a simply truth about me. Most days I maintained my junkie schedule but I could push the envelope and if past actions predicted future events I was in trouble.

Chapter 73

It proved to be an interesting week, but Friday came, the manager's meeting ended, and my assistant manager returned. He had new ideas, understood the products better and had been taught some tricks of the trade. I was happy to have him back and to pay them for their hard work in his absence I gave each of my salesmen a day off with pay. I then set myself up for a vacation by showing my assistant how to work a split shift. I turned the store over to him knowing full well that all I was going to do was heroin.

My assistant had absorbed everything he had learned at the manager's meeting and he wanted to run the store so I used his enthusiasm for my own pleasure. Let him open, close, order product, fill out payroll. My plan was oh so predictable. Once at home I sank into the waiting arms of heroin and turned my day over to the golden eye.

As it turns out my Divisional Manager had been impressed by my assistant manager and in one of our conversations he asked me what I thought about making him the Greensboro store's new manager.

"He'll jump on it."

"You think he'll mind the drive?"

"I doubt it. You want to tell him or should I?"

"No. It has to come from me. I'm sick of Greensboro's numbers, so I've got to make some changes. Let me fire the Greensboro manager and then I'll promote your assistant. While I'm here we'll inventory the store, do a forensic investigation of its paperwork and then I'll let him take over."

"Okay... Just keep me in the loop. I got promotions to deal with and a salesman to hire."

"We might have to replace some of the Greensboro stores staff."

"I'd let your new manager do that. He's got to learn to fire bad employees and train new ones. If he hits a snag you can help him or he can call me."

"Well, there's no point in putting it off. Tell your assistant manager to meet me at the Greensboro store around lunch on Monday and we'll get started with the inventory."

"Okay. I'll tell him on Saturday and you can do the transfer paperwork when he shows up. I'll need him off my payroll as soon as possible. I'll wait until Friday to place an ad for a new salesman."

"Sounds like a plan. I'll make this happen next week and I'll call you if I need to change anything."

Chapter 74

Once again I had exerted my powers of persuasion over my Divisional Manager and got exactly what I wanted. I knew there was a possibility he would stop by my store before going on to Greensboro but I wasn't to worried about that. I felt like celebrating my most recent con job. I knew he would be in the area for an extended period so I was bound to see him some time over the next two weeks. But for now all I could think about was doing my next hit so I drove my truck to a parking lot behind the store and busied myself with a midday fix.

I pulled the plunger back an inch to give the tar a little room to move and used my lighter to heat it up. I worked the cylinder back and forth until its contents started to move. In and out, a good slow shake. Once the contents were liquefied I pushed the air out of the syringe, chose the vein in my ankle and slowly pushed the heroin into my body. The rush traveled like lightening from my foot to my brain. I was in no hurry to go back into the store so I sat there, watching the clouds, smoking cigarettes.

What I was doing was risky at best, some would say insane. Nobody does heroin in plain view. Parked in a bar's parking lot was not exactly hiding but I was a fixture in this neighborhood. So I sat there until I was somewhat stable and then pulled my truck back around front. Once inside I told everybody that we were going to inventory the store. I needed to be accurate and get it done in two days, three at the most. I put each salesmen to work in specific areas and then took my assistant manager outback.

When I told him he had been picked to manage the Greensboro store he had said; "Wow... that was fast. I wasn't expecting it to happen that quick."

"Well, that's why I sent you to the manager's meeting. Greensboro has been a thorn in our Divisional Manager's side for a long time. He's ready to make a change in that store's manager and the first thing he'll want is a complete inventory of the store and a detailed look at its paperwork. This will give you an accurate place to start. Shake out the cobwebs, make sure no skeletons are hiding in the paperwork. That's why we are going to do a complete inventory of this store. I want you to do it like a manager."

"How long will the Divisional Manager stay?"

"All week maybe two. He's going to make sure that you can cut the books, prepare a bank deposit, fill out an inventory order form, hire a new salesman or two and effectively manage your employees. You will find that product knowledge is your number one asset. That store has potential but you're going to have to let our Divisional Manager know you are willing to do what it takes to turn that store around."

"It's a lot to take in at one time."

"I know. But don't worry. I'm always a phone call away. I'll help you with anything. For now just learn to manage the inventory process. I'm going to let you run this one. You've got two salesmen. Use them. This inventory doesn't really count but if you find any discrepancies fix them. It will be the first thing you do at your new store. Let's see how accurate you can be. If you can find anything wrong make it right. Correct any mistakes you find and we'll start the future from there."

I've begun evaporating
Right before your eyes
I just keep regurgitating
My own demise

I miss the day, I miss the past
I miss my veins 'cause they collapse
A simple thought occurs to me

I'm faced down on the tracks
The train is coming fast and it's not
derailing. It's not the first time
And this won't be the last time
That my heart is failing

As the blood is rushing to my
Head from my wrist
I'm in love with all the things
I know I should resist

And all the times you said to me
that falling down is destiny
A simple thought occurs to me

I'm faced down on the tracks
The train is coming fast and
You're right there waiting
It's not the first time
And this won't be the last time
that my heart is failing

Sixx A.M. The Heroin Diaries: Heart Failure
Darren Jay Ashba, James Michael, Nikki Sixx
Lyrics © Warner Chappell Music Inc.
Downtown Music Publishing LLC
Sixx Gunner Music

Chapter 75

There's a lot to be said for mastering the art of deception. It is a delicate skill that takes years to perfect and for a heroin addict it is an essential weapon in their arsenal of distraction. Nobody can ever know the real you. Nobody can ever find out about your addiction. Every move you make must be carefully thought out in order to insure that you're not accidentally revealed. When your world revolves around heroin, deception is the Moon in your Sun. The two go hand in hand.

Your love of heroin is the greatest secret of all. Nobody can ever know. Getting caught is synonymous with being torched by a solar flare. It's like being drug out of the darkness of your personal opium den into the broad daylight where you are guaranteed to melt like wax on a hot stove. Getting caught spells failure and that is never good.

Heroin takes the art of deception to a whole new level. On this new level, deception is a skill honed to perfection by a master deceiver. In the hands of an accomplished deceiver, the lie is a very effective tool. It can be subtle or bold depending on the need of the deceiver. It has to be perceived as real to be effective. The deceiver must be believable and he must present his lie with the same conviction that he would present the truth. He has got to sell his lie as if it were the truth and the best way to do this is for the deceiver to convince himself that what he's saying is, in fact, true.

In doing so he creates a reality that is a subtle blend between the world of heroin and the world of every day people, which as previously stated, is an almost impossible thing to do. To make this type of deceit work the deceiver must weave threads of truth and deception into a story that is easy to remember and just a little bit boring. This is not the time or place for theatrics. Keep it boring. Nothing needs to stand out as unusual. The more details you provide the harder it is for you to keep up with your grand illusion and therefore greater the possibility of you tripping over the facts of your story.

If this happens your deceit will be revealed and your world will fall apart. For a functioning junkie this type of deception is essential to his very survival. He learns to wear it like a second skin. In addition to a well crafted legend the addict must also have the ability to create false schedules, fictitious people as well as places and appointments that don't exist. These are all used for a single purpose. To steal time from a day, a place or a person for the sole purpose of doing heroin. To do this the addict must be able to remember every lie he's ever told. This is a hard thing to do. So you learn to say the same thing over and over. You limit the people you tell and then you tell them only as much as they need to know.

This way they all hear the same story and you come up smelling like roses should they ever decide to compare notes. You can say it's an angle but what you mean is it's a lie. For junkies everything is an angle. You focus on supply, demand and time. This is how you preserve you're relationship with the drug, which of course is the most important thing in your life. So you fabricate a world of illusion to keep from being caught and you keep it simple so that you can remember it without trying.

This means that you must tell your story the same way each and every time. It means that you must be prepared to tell certain portions of your story as it relates to a specific conversation, a specific schedule, a specific person or a specific location. As long as you can maintain the illusion you're safe. Nobodies the wiser, you're skillfully spinning all your plates. For that moment in time you're the master of your universe. But it never last.

You get too many plates spinning at one time and its hard to pay each of them the attention they need. One plate wobbles and crashes to the floor, then another and before you know it your world is falling apart and you have no control over its collapse. All you're left with is a shattered world and the memory that for a brief period you are able to keep your secrets out of sight and your plates spinning beautifully.

Chapter 76

Once again I amazed myself. I wove my way through their world as if I controlled everything. But all the while I was numb. I could feel the junk in my brain, causing my surroundings to come through in waves. Their lips moved but I couldn't hear what they were saying. Was I really that good at hiding my buzz? The best I could hope for was that they didn't know what they were looking at. I had to be high to function and I had to make sure nobody knew the real me. It was quite a balancing act.

At the same time I was taking greater and greater chances. The Divisional Manager entanglement I so boldly flirted with was something I should have avoided. I should have left well enough alone and let my job performance speak for itself. Instead I had acted foolishly and the control of my environment slipped from my grasp. Everything became a case of maybes. Maybe I could drive. Maybe I could get home. Maybe nobody would see that I was stoned out of my mind. Maybe I was finding new ways to cover my drug use. Heroin had hard wired this type of secrecy into my brain at an early age and now I used it with all the skill of an expert.

But my situation was a bit more complicated than that. My heroin addiction was always on the verge of being out of control. I spent every waking minute either dealing with my last hit or thinking about my next one. I was beginning to skip out on work. I was good at making up excuses and my latest had been the stores fledgling contractor business. But I had never went contractor hunting. Not once.

Instead, I created false contractor files and used false contractors to escape the store in favor of heroin. But the golden eye didn't care what I gambled or wagered on its behalf and it was quick to whisper in my brain; "Tear another hole. See if I care. I can make you hurt. I can make you bleed."

Heroin can't love you. I knew that. But it didn't stop me from shooting junk all afternoon. I milked each shot and deliberately overlapped my hits. I pushed myself closer and closer to the line separating life from death and I didn't mind shooting right up to the edge. Maybe it wasn't my time to die. I had not yet reduced myself to the promised puff of smoke and powder. So I kept my rigs loaded. I always had a bullet in the chamber. Give me some time. A week, maybe a month. I'd pull the trigger on an overdose. Commit the perfect self inflicted murder.

Chapter 77

But for now I was safe and with my assistant manager managing a bogus store inventory I was free to do as I pleased. So I went home and prepared myself three one third of a rig hits that I could spend the rest of the day doing. I still had a good buzz from the hit I had taken at the store but a little more would make it just a little better so I did a third and spent the next few hours nodding in and out. This was the best part of heroin. The journey out and in.

It was an experience you couldn't get anywhere else. Between hits I tried to rationalize my situation. I knew that heroin was destroying my connection to Color Tile. Before heroin, my store had been run by me. Now my store was being run by my assistant manager. I was staring at my job through the haze of heroin and I was close to losing it all. My relationship with Color Tile was slowly losing its importance. Everything was being controlled by the monster.

I had reached that point in my addiction where it was only a matter of time before I lost everything. I was breaking my own rules. Now I was trying to make each fix a little better than the one before it and that was a sure fire recipe for destruction. But I wasn't thinking that way so I spent Thursday afternoon stumbling from one fix to the next and finally succumbed to the abuse a little after midnight. I slept until 10AM and got up knowing I had the day off. All I had to do was pick up my paycheck and score.

So I turned to my addiction. I had done it so many times it was like a ritual. It just came naturally. A spoon, some tar, a little water and some fire. Cook it until it boiled, stir it until it was a golden brown soup, then strain that through a filter to produce three one-third rigs and a rinse shot, which I decided to do right away It wasn't much and I had promptly backed it up with a standard one-third hit.

It was an out of body experience. Two shots back to back was a mistake. When the heroin exploded in my brain I fell forward, rolled off the bed and landed on the floor, face up. There was no regret, no sense of alarm, no realization that I had done too much. I felt myself separate from my body and float upward toward the ceiling. I could see my body lying there, syringe hanging out of my arm.

But I was paralyzed. I couldn't see myself clearly. I wasn't sure I was breathing. Heroin hovered like a cloud between me and my body and while that should have been a matter of great concern it wasn't. I remember the idea that "this may be the end" floating by. I didn't want my parents to know that their son had died from a heroin overdose. I needed to get back. I needed to rejoin my physical body. But smack had carried me away and there was nothing I could do.

When I came back was not an issue. It could be a couple of hours from now, sometime this afternoon, sometime tonight. Tomorrow. Maybe never. I had no control over what was happening and I remember thinking that I was close to that promised puff of smoke and powder. I had already became someone I didn't recognize and I was moving closer and closer to being dead. But then slowly, over the next four hours I did come back. I saw myself from miles away and then I sensed myself hovering over my body. I descended into my body and felt myself breathing again. I slowly moved my arms and legs. I was a long way from sober but I wasn't dead. My mind reeled, my plight was obvious.

Chapter 78

I wake up every morning thinking about heroin. I breath in and breath out thinking about heroin. I feel my heart beat thinking about heroin. I stare up at the ceiling thinking about heroin. I step out my front door thinking about heroin. I count cars on the highway thinking about heroin. At work all I do is think about heroin. On my days off all I do is heroin. For a heroin addict to live he's got to fail at what he's doing. If junkies don't get clean they die and they generally do it pretty fast. It only takes one shot too many or a shot that was hotter than you intended.

When my death finally hits the obituaries it will be about heroin. I had gave serious thought to writing my own obituary. I wanted everybody to know the monster I had bravely fought for all these years. I wanted everybody to know that I had went down swinging. It wasn't even 10 AM and already my day was about heroin. My backyard was on fire and I had turned to the golden eye for help. I should have seen that eye for the arsonist it truly was, but I loved it so much I couldn't see the truth.

Instead it had plowed into me at top speed. It didn't feel like an overdose, it felt like death. Once back it took another two hours for me to pull myself into a sitting position and another hour just to stand up. I was eventually able to walk but I was a long way from driving so I wobbled to the laundry room and called the store to see if the mail had brought our checks. My assistant manager said they had so I told him I'd be by later to pick mine up. I also asked him how the inventory had went and he said; "perfect."

"Okay. I'm going to swing by and pick up my paycheck. If I miss you today I'll see you tomorrow."

Chapter 79

I hung the phone up and walked back to the apartment. I got dressed, went by the store for my check, then to the bank for cash, by Wendy's for lunch and the liquor store for vodka. Once back at home I ate a few fries, a bite of hamburger and an apple pie. It wasn't much but it was something. I sat back, with a cigarette in hand, and thought about last night. For the second time in as many weeks I crossed the line and somehow, miraculously, made it back without suffering irreparable damage. One thing was certain. If I didn't dial things back a notch I was gonna die.

I took a shower and drove over to Happy Hills. I found my dealer and we nodded to each other as I pulled up. We shared a muted familiarity. I needed a good to make it through the next two weeks and he had agreed to sell me ten packs for the price of eight. He said something about quantity getting me a deal and I had handed him four one-hundred dollar bills in exchange ten packets which he tossed on the seat, counting as he went. He then slapped my truck door and said; "giddy up little doggy."

I pulled away wondering how long it would take for the heroin in me to evaporate and withdrawal to start tearing me apart? How long before smack became the only thing on my mind? How long before junk became my only option? I made it back home just as my guts started knotting up and pretty soon my nerves were on fire. Sweating and shaking. As it turns out withdrawing from good heroin comes on you just as fast as its rush. But I had prepared rigs at the ready so I quickly satisfied the monster.

That was the last of my prepared hits so I set myself to

making three more. I worked my way through the process and ended up with a beautiful golden eye the size of a tablespoon. It was a lot of processed heroin and I remember thinking that there had to be at least five hits in that spoon. So I dropped a piece of cotton into the mix and prepared six rigs, one-third full each. It was a lot of prepared heroin. Enough to last me two days.

Chapter 80

In fact, I stayed so high that I couldn't have worked Saturday if I wanted to. I called the store with some flimsy excuse and then spent the day in a heroin fog, not really abusing myself, just keeping my buzz at a level I could enjoy without being totally knocked out. This was safe abuse and for a junkie like me it was pretty good control. 8 PM came and went. Midnight passed without complaint. At 6 AM Sunday the golden eye came calling and I was ready.

I liquefied the last of my prepared rigs and got my day off to a smooth start. It was an enjoyable buzz and since Sunday was the third day of this heroin inspired trifecta I turned my attention to preparing its poison. I processed my dope and then sat my spoon down on the counter and prepared two rigs, half full each. These were hot shots but I had all day. Around lunch I liquefied one of them and tried to fire it. however there was no veins in my left hand. So I tried my the left ankle but its veins were gone too.

That left me with only one possibility; hit a vein in my right arm. I was not very good at shooting left handed, however I wanted the rush so I did what I had to do. I wrapped my tourniquet around my upper right arm and pulled it tight. A nice healthy vein popped up. This is where I needed to be and I wasted no time hitting it. When I saw blood in the chamber I fired the entire load and released the tourniquet.

The rush was almost too much. These large loads were dangerous and when I did them I couldn't help but think of Ricky. At this moment I wanted a big hit. I wanted to blow the top of my head off. I wanted heroin that would propel me into the heavens, to roll me over like a train. I wasn't afraid of heroin and that was a very dangerous position to be in. Either one of these hot shots could easily kill me.

Every half an hour or so I took a drink off my vodka. Several hours later, while still high I got my next hit ready. I wanted a bullet in the chamber so I danced my little dance, rinsed my spoon with vodka and then added enough water to make a shot. I used fire and my rig's plunger to dissolve the contents of my spoon, drew everything into my rig and thumped the air out of it. It turned out to be three-quarters of a rig. I was amazed. I had done a good job cleaning up my spoon but this shot should be too weak.

At the same time it looked good. It was from the same small piece of tar I had now gotten three hits off of. The first hit off this piece had scared the hell out of me and my mind was telling me that a rig three-quarters full from the same spoon would probably kill me. So I returned enough of it to the spoon to reduce it to half. Through the fog I imagined the smack in my rig to be a bullet in a gun, waiting to be fired into my brain. I laid the syringe on the night-stand, stretched out on the bed and went to sleep.

When I awoke seven hours later it was half past midnight. The rig I had fixed earlier was sitting there, patiently waiting for me. All it needed was a little heat and a careful shake. I lite my candle and began running the rig over its flame. I worked the plunger back and forth, making sure the cylinder did not overheat. Liquefying a cold rig is a delicate process, one wrong move, one minor distraction would melt the rig. If you opened the rig's wall you would lose you're whole load. If you just melted the rig you could retrieve the heroin inside but it was a waste of a good rig.

Chapter 81

Once ready I wrapped my tourniquet around my lower right arm and pulled it tight. After a couple of seconds a vein on top of my hand stood up and I was able to slide my needle in. The heroin exploded in my brain and coursed through my body like the poison I knew it to be. This hit was as strong as the last one. My arms and legs were numb. The heroin fog rolled in. I wasn't holding back or compensating for what my dealer called "fresh and strong." I was enjoying his heroin to the fullest.

For me heroin this good was better than money. This kind of thinking was insane and inspired by the golden eye who whispered in my ear, "you're gonna die." But my wicked, irrational mind suggested that I had found the perfect formula. Divide a single packet into two equal pieces. Each one created a liquefied spoonful of smack that was divided into three equal shots. It was brilliant. Morning, noon and night with a rinse shot to finish off the day. This made a single pack last two days.

So why couldn't I stick to the formula? Sunday proved to be a repeat of Saturday. By 6 PM I had shot four large loads and spent the whole day in heroin's warm, carefree embrace. Not a new record, but still worth noting. Sunday night came soon enough and I knew I had to start getting my shit together. The next few weeks were going to test my metal.

My assistant manager was moving to Greensboro as its new manager so I had to promote my lead salesman and train him to be my assistant. I also had to hire a new salesman, which meant interviewing applicants. Once hired my new man would have to be trained, but that task could easily be handled by my assistant manager. This approach would let me teach the assistant manager every aspect of running a retail store, particularly its many reports and that was certainly doable over a two week period.

But I was getting ahead of myself and so around 9 PM I prepared a small hit and fired into my right arm on the first try. I cleaned out my rig and stretched out on the bed to enjoy the buzz. The buzz that always got you high. Floating free in a state of perfect silence, high above the concerns of the world. It never lasted long enough and coming down was hell. That's why it was nice to overlap hits. Don't wait until you're jonesing to do your next shot. Keep enough heroin in your system at all times. Don't ever come down. With that pearl of wisdom fresh in my brain I went to sleep and slept until 6 AM.

Chapter 82

The first thing I did upon waking was prepare three third of a rig hits. I don't know why I couldn't see it but I had became a slave to heroin. I shot the first one immediately and cleaned the syringe for future use. I put the caps back on the remaining rigs and carefully wrapped them in a washcloth. With my old assistant gone I was going to have to work some long days. But I knew my split shift idea would work and my established staff had seen it in action so they were fine with it. My plan was to have my new assistant up and running by the end of the week so that he could train my new salesman.

I promoted my top salesman to assistant store manager the minute he punched in and started teaching him the store's paperwork. We worked on it three days nonstop, either studying old reports or doing new ones. It took three days of up close, personal training but he was a quick study and after watching him complete Wednesday's paperwork on his own I patted him on the back and said; "Congratulations, you are now my assistant manager. Here's your keys. You open the store every day and leave at 5PM. I come in at noon and leave to 8PM. I have Friday and Sunday off, you have Sunday and Monday off."

It had taken three quick days to train him and during that time my split shift approach had been perfect. I shot my first load before leaving home, met him at 8 AM and we trained until I left at noon. I fixed myself at home and returned to oversee his daily paperwork. I sent him home around 5 PM and closed the store at 8 PM. My last fix happened around nine every evening and this had made for perfect days as well as descent nights. All I had to do now was hire a new salesman and I placed an ad in the local newspaper Thursday morning. With any luck I'd have a new employee by the following week.

Chapter 83

When I got home I found the last rig I had prepared that morning and busied myself liquefying it. I had started using my right arm several weeks back and while doing so was still awkward I had gotten good enough to insert my rig, check for blood and slowly push the poison into my arm. The hit was instant. I was barely able to pull the rig out of my arm. I was whisked away by the soft, sweet, silence brought to those who worshiped at heroin's altar. Floating free. No fear, or cares, just perfect peace and quiet.

An interesting thing was now happening in my brain. Thanks to my heroin warped mind I was always looking for ways to avoid Color Tile. I could not afford to get close to anyone. I had my new assistant manager doing all the store's paperwork because my mind didn't work like it once did. However it was sharp enough to perpetrate my latest trick. I bought a brief case and set up a phony contractor business. I filled it with the store's contractor files, graph paper, old blue prints, business cards, a couple ink pens, pencils, a calculator and a tape measure. My contractor business was up and running. It looked real and it required weekly maintenance. I had to beat the bushes. Who knows where I might have to go. I might actually find one, at home, lying on my bed, with a needle in my arm.

Another issue that had me living dangerously was the fact that I carried a couple of half full rigs with me everywhere I went. I shot heroin before I went to work, while I was at work, and when I got home. I drove high, worked high, couldn't sleep unless I was high. This kind of abuse was going to result in disaster but in my mind I was untouchable. When I was at home

I shot at will. On my days off I did the same. I don't know how I managed to carry on as long as I did but somehow I always got up on time and I always made it to work on time. This routine lulled me into a false sense of security. I was slowly but surely destroying myself. My addiction was out of control. I was spending eight hundred dollars a month on junk. That was sixteen packs for an average of one packet every two days, three hits a day.

Chapter 84

Still that wasn't enough to satisfy the bottomless pit my addiction had become. I had cut every none essential thing from my life. So to generate cash I decided to sell my living room furniture including a couch, coffee table, two end tables and a four piece entertainment set. The entertainment set held my T.V., my stereo and had shelves for books as well as a fold down desk. My neighbor had always been interested in it so when I asked him if he wanted to buy it for six hundred dollars he said "yes." He also bought my T.V., and my stereo for four-hundred dollars. I had helped him move all four pieces to his apartment and we put it together. We added the T.V., and stereo and I netted one-thousand dollars cash.

I posted a "for sale" notice in the laundry room and within days I sold the couch, coffee table and end tables for another four hundred dollars. This totaled fourteen-hundred dollars cash. The only thing on the ground floor was two lawn chairs. It didn't matter. My primary interest was upstairs and that got me thinking. I could save even more money by downsizing to a one bedroom apartment. So I walked over to the office and asked if I could move into a one bedroom apartment. The manager had said sure, so I picked an apartment, transferred my lease and moved in.

Looking back I can honestly say that I did it all for heroin. I turned off my utilities for heroin. Stopped bar hopping for heroin. Sold everything I owned to finance heroin. I had downsized my apartment for heroin. I spent three-quarters of my monthly salary on heroin. I took this liquidation windfall and went to my dealer. Twenty-eight packets for fourteen hundred dollars. A one time deal that definitely lined my pockets and if I kept buying once a month I would never run out. Having this much heroin was a dream come true but it also came with a death sentence.

Chapter 85

You know how they say, "it takes one-hundred at-ta boys to get over one o-shit?" Well that's the way it worked for me. As far as I knew everything was going well in Greensboro. I hadn't heard anything that would suggest otherwise and I had my own store to run, so I figured no news was good news. However I was wrong. My old assistant manager wasted no time trying to score brownie points by ratting me out to our Divisional Manager. He had said that he didn't know exactly what – he couldn't actually be sure – but something told him I was on drugs.

At first my Divisional Manager had brushed his claim aside by saying; "That's impossible. He's the best manager I've got. Have you ever seen him do drugs?"

"No... its just a feeling I get. He runs his store perfectly, but I think he's high on something."

"Well if that's the case he's doing a better job high than most of my store manager's are doing sober."

But the seed of doubt had been planted and my Divisional Manager couldn't stop thinking about it. He stayed in Greensboro for two weeks auditing the store's books and inventorying its stock. He found the store in such poor condition that he fired the entire staff, officially made my assistant its new manager and together they had hired a new sales crew. He spent a week training this new staff and was amazed by what my assistant manager knew. In the end he was very pleased with the way I had trained him.

Still, he could not get my former employees words out of his mind. He should have known that the new manager would seek to endear himself with something like this but he had fell for it and he wanted to see me face to face. So instead of calling he stopped by on his way back to Charlotte. I was sitting at my desk doing paperwork and I didn't hear him come in. So when he knocked on the sales counter he startled me and I jumped in my chair; "Damn man. We need to get you some squeaky shoes."

"Just stopping by to check on your sales. How did you do today?"

"I did good, sold one contractor three-thousand square foot of ceramic tile, as well as thin set and grout. I don't have that much in stock so I ordered what he needed to insure lot numbers. We had a lot of little sales, mom and pop stuff. I sent one salesman home early and let the other one handle those."

"Good, I'm impressed with my new manager. You did a good job training him but I do have some bad news. He stabbed you in the back the first chance he got. Accused you of doing drugs... of coming to work high... of doing drugs while you're at work. Is that true?"

I looked at my Divisional Manager and sarcastically replied, "Look around. My store's perfect because I know what I'm doing. As you have seen my employees are properly trained. My sales increase year over year." My angle was simple; blow up in his face. Back him off by acting insulted. Be outrageous. It was the only chance I had. "Look at this place. It's picture perfect. You should be ashamed. A new manager, hired by me, trained by me, with no management experience, is messing with your head."

But my Divisional Manager had me dead to right; "I can tell you're high on something."

He was right about that. I was all over the map. In the twinkling of an eye heroin destroyed my career. There was no mistaking my buzz. I stuttered and swayed from side to side. I gritted my teeth, lost my train of thought, nodded in and out. Just for a second, every now and then, but that's all it took.

When lucid I continued defending myself, but I didn't help my cause. "Inventory this store, you'll find my paperwork is perfect. Everything is up to date. I send you a weekly report and

I'm up fifteen percent year over year and that's no guess. I'm growing this business like no other manager in this division."

"I know. And I know when I'm being played. There's only one way to ease my mind. Take a drug test."

"That's not necessary."

"Its not a request. It's mandatory. I'll set it up at Prime Care and we'll go from there. If you test positive I won't have much choice. You're a great manager but the company has a no drug's policy. I'll do every thing I can to help you but ultimately I've got no control over it."

"You've got some control. Don't order the test. Just turn around and walk away. Forget it."

"He turned to look at me and that instant glance told the tale. I now hated him and he no longer trusted me. Our professional relationship was over and where camaraderie had once been, a wall now stood. We would never speak kindly to one another again. I was still employed by Color Tile but that was just a matter of paperwork. I knew my job was over and without seeing the drug test he knew it to.

Chapter 86

I wasn't clean by any stretch of the imagination and I knew it. I didn't know much about the physiology of heroin and I didn't know who to ask. I had heard it metabolized rapidly. Someone had said four days and I had heard seven. If I could put twenty-four hours between my last shot and the drug test would I pass? Or would it take weeks to piss clean? My last hit had been around 5 PM. If I stopped now could I make it eighteen hours without a fix? I seriously doubted it. And I was right. I closed the store as soon as my Divisional Manager left and spent the next two hours sanitizing my files. I was a few days ahead on my paperwork so I had to re-figure everything.

It was tedious work and before I knew it I was withdrawing. One more day and my paperwork would be perfect. Then all that would be left was my heroin contaminated piss. My Divisional Manager had destroyed my world with a random drug test and now I would do the only thing I could think of. I tried drinking a pint of vodka and eating ten Xanax but it didn't help. I drank another pint and took ten more Xanax. Nothing changed. Slowly jonesing, turned into dope sick and I had no choice but to fix a small shot and satisfy the monster.

I then went to bed and had a terrible night. I tossed and turned. In my dream's I was fighting. Around two in the morning I started gagging and shortly thereafter I started vomiting. There was precious little inside of me to throw up so puking turned to retching and then the dry heaves. I exhausted my guts. It felt like I was being torn apart. There was nothing left to do. I took a long hot shower and when hot water didn't work I tried cold water. A cold shower might wake you up but when your jonesing, and you know what you need is in the next room, the pain is beyond measure.

I toweled off, redressed my arm, got ready for work and laid back down. At 6 AM I began a slow count down. I needed to wait as long as possible which meant arriving at Prime Care some time around 11:45 AM. My entire body was screaming for heroin. About seven o'clock I fixed three rigs, all half shot hits, and sat there trembling. I was beginning to exhibit the symptoms of withdrawal. Fragile doesn't even begin to describe how I felt. But 10 AM came, then 11 AM and then it was time to go to Prime Care.

I got there a little before twelve and waited fifteen minutes for my name to be called. After about ten minutes of trying I was able to fill the little cup about half way. That was all they were going to get. I drove from Prime Care to Color Tile, parked behind the building and liquefied one of my rigs. God how I needed this fix. And the veins in my right arm agreed. They were all standing nice and tall so I eased my rig into the largest one and emptied it. My body instantly gave thanks. I sat there flying in the feather white skies that can only be found when looking at the world through heroin tinted glasses.

Chapter 87

For the next few days my addiction and job were business as usual. Sales were slow, my need for junk was at an all time high and I was sending employees home early just to keep them away from me. That resulted in lower labor cost which let me fax good numbers despite slow sales. If you looked at the numbers it looked like I was adjusting payroll to match sales. I wasn't doing it to look smart but it made me look smart and my Divisional Manager had called to compliment me on my precision management. "Did you do the drug test?"

"Sure, did it Monday morning."

"Are you worried about it?"

"I know what it's going to say. I'm doing the best I can. I suffer from chronic insomnia. My sleep is so bad even my doctor can't treat it. I sleep four to six hours every five or so days and that's taking some kind of pill twice a day. My doctor thinks it's brain chemistry but at this point I think that's a guess."

"Why didn't you say something about this the other day. I would probably not have ordered a drug test if I had known about your medical condition."

"A good friend would not have jumped to the conclusion you jumped to. Doesn't matter if you're right or wrong. Sometimes it a matter of having a friends back and you abandoned me."

"I know that's how it looks and this will probably destroy our relationship. I know that. But if you test positive for drugs I'm going to have to let you go. I can't jeopardize my job trying to cover for you."

"All hail the conquering fool." This was the second time I had heard his crap in twenty-four hours and I didn't feel like hearing it again. So I hung up on him. I didn't care. If I wasn't worth saving who was? If he couldn't make an exception for the best store manager he had who could he make an exception for? Like he said; "I was the best manager he had." Fuck him. What's the worse thing he could do, fire me?

Chapter 88

The following day my Divisional Manager received my drug test and of course the test was positive for opiates. He called the lab and the technician told him that the parts per million were very high. I had not helped myself by going fifteen hours without a fix. In fact, it had been a waste of time. My body was saturated with heroin; it was in my bones. It ran through my veins. It colored my skin. I sweated it, tasted it, craved it. I shot it all day long. I spent every dime I could get my hands on buying the stuff.

There was no telling what I would do if I actually ran out. I might go criminal; go back to selling drugs. Become a thief. Now my Divisional Manager knew I used an opiate of some kind and he had a decision to make. Fire me or cover it up. After talking to the lab and spending a couple of hours mulling it over he chose to play it by the book. He called to tell me he was letting me go. The only favorable thing he could do was lay me off as an "elimination of position." This would allow me to draw unemployment. He would let me work my shift which would take me to the end of the current pay period.

We would meet the next day so that he could give me my layoff papers and take possession of my keys. That was it. My days at Color Tile were over and waiting for my last day to end was like waiting to be executed at dusk. I finally said "fuck it" logged out and went home. The golden eye had scored big. I had no idea what to do next but the first thing I did was take a quick inventory. I had saved my yearly bonuses for three years running so I had roughly four-thousand dollars in my saving account. I also had close to one-thousand dollars in checking and a couple hundred in my pocket. I had used the fourteen-hundred dollars I made selling my furniture to buy twenty-eight packs and my dealer had gave me seven for buying so much at one time.

I used my last paycheck to buy fifteen additional packs for a grand total of around fifty packets. I had two weeks of pay plus one week of vacation pay coming to me as my final pay check. That was around twenty-five hundred dollars and unemployment would follow so I could manage for a few months.

But it had been a particular stressful day and I wanted to get as far away from it as possible. So I settled onto my bed and went about the process of liquefying a spoon full of heroin. I rested the rig on a small piece of cotton and pulled back on the plunger until the syringe was three-quarters of the way full. I pushed the air out, cleaned the tip of the needle with a little vodka and studied what I had just made. This was a strong, hot shot. This one could easily take my life. But I didn't care. I wanted to get as far away from today as possible and nothing could take me away faster than heroin.

I held the rig with my left hand, found a vein in my right arm and slid the needle into place. I pulled the plunger back just enough to make sure I was in the vein and when I saw blood I pushed the whole load into my arm at one time. As it turns out I had a couple of things working for me and a couple things working against me. For starters, I hadn't ate in twenty-four hours so my stomach was empty. I might have gagged as the heroin flooded my body, but I didn't throw up. I also had a pint of vodka nearby so I was able to take a swallow before sagging back onto the pillows that lined my headboard.

This was the strongest shot I had ever done and I was pushed from my body with force. My heart rate slowed to dangerous levels and my breathing was negligible. For the next two hours I lay there next to dead. Nobody serious about seeing tomorrow would dare shot this much heroin at one time. I had seen people die doing less. I didn't care. I had followed heroin to the brink of death once before and clawed my way back. Now I didn't fear it as much as I should have.

Color Tile had served as a boundary and my job brought in the money that made my heroin addiction possible. During the past two years I had turned heroin into my personal armor and my weapon of self-destruction. I had always said I could run a Color Tile store better blindfolded than most could with an owners manual. My Divisional Manager knew this and he had fired me anyway. Sometimes you bend the rules to protect your assets and he should have done a better job protecting me.

Chapter 89

Maybe it was this continuous line of inebriated, fighting mad, thought that kept me from dying from an intentional overdose. I was mad as hell and could only think about the conversation I had had with my Divisional Manager earlier in the day. Now my world was on fire and I had turned to the golden eye for help. There was simply no denying my denial. I had grown accustomed to having it around. I saw its paraphernalia on a daily basis.

Traveling to Happy Hills was no big deal to me. However others did not have the dulled senses I had and I was well aware of the stigma attached to both heroin and its users. It was the source of a lot of crime, personal pain and death. I was neck deep in this stigma and about to drown. I used heroin several times a day and bought large quantities of it every month. It was people like me who made its illegal sale possible. It was people like me who overdosed and died. Maybe I didn't care. Maybe I didn't see myself as a junkie. Maybe smack was the best thing in my life. The one thing I could count on.

To prove that I had used a large amount of heroin to forget my last day at Color Tile and I had stopped just short of death. It had taken over eight hours to get over my last hit. I had actually slept through the last few hours and I had woke up a little after midnight ready for my next fix. My only schedule was to meet my Divisional Manager at ten-thirty the next morning. That was all I had to do for the foreseeable future. So I pulled another shot from the spoon I had fixed a little earlier and slipped back into darkness of heroin induced unconsciousness.

I awake at 6 AM and after administering a one-third shot I unwrapped my left arm, took a shower, and redressed my arm with fresh bandages. I dressed in crisp, clean clothes and at 10 AM I left to meet my Divisional Manager. We arrived at Color Tile at the same time. I eyed him with great hatred and handed him my keys as well as my contractor brief case. When he saw all I had done to make it look real he said: "Wow. I'm firing the best manager I have because of a failed drug test. I wish there was another way. There's only one thing I can do for you. Instead of outright firing you I'm laying you off. This will let you draw unemployment. Here's your layoff papers and a letter of recommendation. You're a great manager and I know this doesn't mean much to you right now, but I do wish you the best of luck."

As I pulled out of the parking lot I flipped him a bird and turned away to face my uncertain future. We would never see each other again and at the time I didn't care. The one thing I didn't know was that just down the road a store named The Home Depot was breaking ground on a 125,000 square foot hardware store and indoor lumber yard. They sold everything you could image for construction work and this included an extensive line of flooring choices; ceramic and marble, wall tile of every kind. A multitude of wood applications and the setting materials to install anything you wanted at prices that could not be beat. Within twelve months The Home Depot had put my Color Tile store out of business and within two years they would kill off the entire chain.

Chapter 90

The next day I went to the Employment Security Commission and got my unemployment started. It was a paltry two-hundred and seventy-five dollars a week. Eleven hundred dollars a month for the next six months. That was roughly half my Color Tile salary. But for now I had a brief period during which I could do as much heroin as I dared, as many times a day as I could mix a fix and find a vein. I was free to indulge my addiction and if I died, well I just died. Death had touched my life so many times.

It had ripped cherished friends people from my life. Torn two beautiful lovers from my side, This was, in large part, why I lusted after the golden eye. You couldn't hurt it, it wouldn't die and from the looks of it, it wasn't going anywhere. I was amazed to still be alive. Most people in my position would have ran screaming to their doctor. Me? I ran screaming to my dealer and bought ten more packs of heroin.

I had made his day on more than one occasion and while I had plenty it was comforting to know that I could make this purchase. At this point there was no sense in denying it. I was a junkie. Totally alone. No friends, no drinking buddies. I hadn't seen my family in almost three years. Before pulling away I told my dealer; "Next week I'll buy twenty packs. I'm gonna need a good deal."

"Okay. I'll be here. I'll cut you a break. But I'm telling you man; you're killing yourself. I've watched you go from healthy and handsome to a walking, talking skeleton. I don't want to lose you. You're one of my best customers. But you need to give yourself a break. It would be a shame to see you die."

Chapter 91

  With his words fresh on my mind I drove straight back to the apartment, tossed my twelve new packs into my bedside drawer and turned my attention to the one I was working on. It was all so systematic. If I was lucky I could get a quick fix by rinsing my spoon. But ultimately it came down to a shot straight off the block. There was a reason for making three hits at a time. You wouldn't lose dope if you fix all of them while you were clear headed and somewhat sober. If you're not careful you can turn your spoon over, or boil it over. Or you're timing will turn into the shakes and that makes it hard not to spill a shot.

  But, if all goes well, your conservation efforts will pay off with no lost smack. You will consume every speck from every block from every tin foil packet. Conservation is the sign of a perfect heroin user. On the other hand, frequency is a killer and eventually that happens to every addict. Something keeps you from your schedule and the next thing you know your jonesing. Then your sick. You shake and tremble, hot and cold. Your stomach flip flops between gut wrenching knots and electro-shock therapy.

  Every nerve in your body feels like its on fire. You fix a hit as soon as you can, as strong as possible and that's all it takes. That single shot, under those circumstances, will kill you. On the other hand, if you try to quit cold turkey the shook to your system would be enough to kill you. If you were serious about quitting and you want to stop comfortably, then Methadone is highly recommended.

  At this point none of these issues concerned me. I had more heroin than sense and I treated each packet with all the sensitivity of a lover. Hold it gently, folded its foil back, corner by corner, side by side until it lay there, naked and exposed. One healthy square of black tar heroin. Now break off a little piece and drop it in your spoon. Wet it down with a little vodka and crush it with your plunger. Add some water, lite your candle and let the flame bring your lover to a boil. Use your plunger to crush and stir the mix into a tablespoon of beautiful brown soup; the ever present golden eye.

Drop in a piece of cotton and sit the sharp end on it. Pull your rig three quarters full then reverse it and thump out the air bubbles. Just a slow, gentle thump and a slow push upwards until there was no more bubbles in your rig. Then rinse the point and hit a vein. This was the only point in the process where I had trouble. My left arm was off limits. I had to choose between my left ankle, or my right arm. Both areas were beginning to show signs of abuse but I needed my arms to look as clean as possible.

So I used my belt as a tourniquet just above my ankle. It was a descent vein but it was deep and painful to hit. If I missed I would try my right arm, but I had hit it perfectly and emptied my syringe. The hit exploded in my head and touched every nerve in my body with tender peace and numbing kindness.

I cleaned up my rig, capped it and laid it on my plate. I blew out the candle and laid back. Not to much, not to little. Perfect. I felt absolutely marvelous. I could stay this way forever. Then again that was the kind of thinking that got me here in the first place. I nodded comfortably in and out for several hours and came down ready to do it all again. I had no place to be, no schedule to maintain, so I danced with the devil with all the clarity of a dream.

Chapter 92

I regained control of my faculties sometime around midnight and dutifully prepared my next fix. I was on a roll and went for my next fix like it was my last. I needed to eat something and redress my arms. I wasn't sure what day it was, so doing it "tomorrow" was as good as I could get. For now, for that very minute, all I wanted was my next fix. This one would get me through the night and I had followed the procedure that took me from wanting it to having it.

I slept through the night and woke up around 5 AM. I felt neutral. Neither jonesing nor hungry. Neither ragged nor rested. It was a rare moment and I used it to change out the bandage on my left arm. This was a process I knew by heart and from all I could tell it was helping. There were rows of small red dots tracing each vein from my wrist to my elbow but all the bruising was gone as was the swelling.

I left the bandage off, reasoning that fresh air would do it some good and once done I walked outside to smoke a cigarette. I didn't have to many quirks but one of them was smoking indoors. I didn't like the smell that lingered and it didn't take long for that smell to get into everything. When I lived in the town house I had smoked inside and I think that's where I developed my dislike of the odor.

Some quirks make sense and some don't. I didn't like the smell a cigarette left behind but apparently I didn't mind the things heroin left behind. Like my emaciated remains, my mincemeat arms, my not so fresh body odor, my overall crumpled look. I hadn't showered in weeks and my one objection was the smoke of a cigarette. Strange... for someone killing themselves with heroin, that was strange.

I lite another cigarette and watched the sunrise thinking that for a normal person, today would have meaning. Something to do, somewhere to go, something to remember. For me the Sun was rising and I was dying. I would spend today in a darkness of my own making. Drifting from fix to fix. I wouldn't enjoy the fresh air, wouldn't experience the Sun's warmth, or the company of friends who had long forgotten me. My only companion was the golden eye and because of that eye I would spend my day in the dark. Just me, vodka and junk. I was skinny as a rail and shot full of holes. But the golden eye cunningly whispered; "Everything will be okay – Everything will be alright."

Chapter 93

As days turned into weeks my ability to protect myself grew weaker and weaker. Heroin was devouring me and I was powerless to stop it. Nothing proved its control more than the fact that I spent the next month shooting heroin non-stop. I was predictable and regimented. Every four hours until both ankles bled and my right arm looked like it had been stabbed repeatedly with a fork. I had even started using the veins on the top of my left hand because they were coming back into view.

I spent a second month shooting heroin non-stop. I had no job so I had nothing to do, nothing to hide, and nowhere to go. I was in self-destruct mode. Without intervention my worthless life could end at any time. It could happen today or with any shot I choose. Each hit weakened me, made it easier for heroin to kill me and leave nothing in its wake but a puff of powder and smoke. One day I remember thinking I was hungry and for something different I ordered a pizza.

When I opened the door the delivery boy gasped and took a step backward. He looked like he had seen a ghost. I paid him and he couldn't get away fast enough. What had scared him? Me? I sat the pizza on the counter and walked into the bathroom. What I saw in the mirror scared me. I was ghostly pale, blue with a scraggly beard. My skin was drawn tight across my face giving it an eerie, reflective glow. Add my bandaged arm to this equation and I looked like a scarecrow that had been left out in the rain.

So I took a long, hot shower. I hadn't showered for a couple months because I didn't have anywhere to go and to be honest, when you're cruising from fix to fix its easy to lose track of time. But a fresh change of clothes helped and a couple pieces of pizza had filled my stomach and made me sleepy. So I stretched out on the bed and slept a couple of hours. But it wasn't long before heroin came knocking and mercilessly pulled me from my bed.

It was unrelenting and could wear you thin. I might go to bed resting easy from my latest shot but when it ran dry it was like being pushed through a whirling blender. I had learned to take all this in stride. Everything I needed was within reach and my night time shots were almost mechanical. I'm not saying I could shoot heroin in my sleep but sometimes I fixed a hit, shot it and nodded off only to wake up hours later with no recollection of that last hit.

All I'd have to remind me of my nocturnal activities would be a crusty spoon, a burnt out candle and a bloody rig. An open flame and an unconscious drug addict was a scary scenario. Sometimes I would do a shot so hot it would take the whole day to get over it and I would actually sleep through the last few hours. I would come to with a small buzz and before jonesing I would fix my next hit. I was living so close to the edge I could peer into the abyss. And you know what they say about starring into the abyss.

For me managing my intake of heroin so that I lived right up to the point of no return was just another good day. Without boundaries of any sort I knew this kind of "good day" over and over and over again. I was now spending the three-thousand dollars I had in savings. The rest of my money was gone. Rent, bills, and repeat trips to Happy Hills cleaned me out. Unemployment was coming in but I spent it fast.

During brief moments of lucidity my mind wandered back to the deaths Melinda and Diane. My heart was shattered and there was no fixing that. My only pain killer was heroin and heroin was killing me. I was in my head and needed a change of scenery. I had been sitting in this apartment in the dark, by myself, way too long. Mentally I was a disaster. My mind was spinning out of control. I was exhausted and going insane.

Completely over the edge. The apartment felt less like a home and more like a tomb.

Chapter 94

I had to get out for a while. Fresh air and a different environment would do me good. It couldn't get any worse. I didn't know what time it was or where I was going and I didn't care. I pulled on a sweat shirt, jeans, tennis shoes, grabbed what little cash I had and two rigs of prepared heroin. I headed into town and stopped at the first bar I came to. I wanted to be among people. Have a couple of drinks. I didn't need friends, just a no name bar with a couple no name people.

I found what I was looking for and once inside I surveyed its inhabitants. Several people were shooting pool, a pair of couples sat at the bar and a pretty young lady, about my age was sitting at the far end of the bar; clearly alone, drinking bourbon. She was pret-ty enough, a little rough around the edges, it was hard to tell in the bar's light. The bourbon was an interest-ing choice but it was her beauty that made her seem out of place. She was a cut above her surroundings. She didn't belong here.

As I moved closer she came into focus and I could tell that she was suffering. She was on the edge of rough. Not just a simple rough but a special rough. I knew this look. She was not just suffering from a hangover, and that bourbon wasn't going to fix anything. What she needed couldn't be found in a bar. I looked at her arms for tracks but she was wearing long sleeves. It was just part of the picture my mind was drawing as I made my way to her side. She reminded me of a beautiful gem, that for some reason was lost and forgotten, alone and abandoned in a rundown bar.

Was someone missing her? She had probably learned to drink bourbon straight while extremely high. She closed her eyes and swayed from side to side, only for a second and as she did she clinched her teeth. She fit the bill. Frail, thin to the point of starvation and positively miserable in her own skin. She needed a fix. For someone like me, who looked at heroin everyday, she was not that big of a mystery.

You may wonder how I could make such a determination on the spot. It's simple. Junkies ignore the population at large and are always looking for other junkies. Regular people wouldn't know a junkie if they saw one. Junkies need our own kind. We're like vampires. We love the dark, blood is a part of our daily craft and we are always looking for fresh souls on which to feed.

And then there is the economic possibility. Other junkies may have heroin or they may have money and be willing to pool resources and score larger than usual amounts. This relationship will last until one or the other had been rung dry and the stronger junkie moves on. If a male junkie finds a very rare female junkie and they connect on a personal level their relationship may last for years. But even in this type of relationship everybody has to pull their own weight and female junkies often trade sex for junk and only heroin will do.

She speaks to me in Persian
Tells me that she loves me,
the girl with golden eyes

And though I hardly know her
I let her in my veins
And trust her with my life.

I wish I had never kissed her
'Cause I just can't resist her
the girl with golden eyes.
Every time she whispers

"Take me in your arms
The way you did last night."

Everything will be okay
And everything will be alright.
If I can get away from her
And save my worthless life.

I wake up every morning
Jonesin' for her love,
the girl with golden eyes.
I won't have to wait long

Till she buries me with roses,
She's always by my side.

Sixx A.M. The Heroin Diaries: Girl with Golden Eyes
Darren Jay Ashba, James Michael, Nikki Sixx
Lyrics © Downtown Music Publishing LLC
Warner Chappell Music Inc.
Sixx Gunner Music

Chapter 95

Okay. Before going any further there's something that needs to be said about me at this particular time in my life. Something that needs to be said about this particular night. For starters, when I made the decision to get out of the apartment I was crazy high and had been on a heroin bender for close to four months. I had lost contact with the outside world and was operating in a state of severe paranoia. To further complicate the situation I brought several rigs full of smack with me. This was a given.

The potential charges were building fast and I was desperate for a change of scenery without changing any part of me. As a result I was breaking my own rules. I was driving crazy high and I didn't know where I was going. I was beginning to think in terms of an hour glass and truthfully it was beginning to feel like I didn't have a lot of time left. These ingredients could easily combine to create a disaster from which I may not recover. But I didn't care. I didn't think of the potential downside to my drug inspired decision because I had been living in a six-hundred square foot cell for seven months.

I lived without emergency backup and felt like I could take care of myself. But there was one element I did not count on and this leads me to the subject at hand. Picking up strays. As a general rule I refuse to pick up strays and the reason is fairly simple. You don't pick up stray dogs because they might have rabies. And you don't pick up stray girls because they might have herpes. In addition, you never know what stray girls might be hiding in their personal baggage. If they're a stray there's always a reason and to be fair it's not always their fault.

There may be troublesome ex-husbands or possessive ex-boyfriends lurking in their past or they might have kids to keep up with. Any of these was a deal breaker for me. I couldn't handle the entanglement. Another issue for me was the fact that their habits would probably not match up with mine. Nothing looks worse on a woman than Jim Beam. Then again I shouldn't complain because I'm pretty sure my friends wouldn't approve of the way I wore heroin. Like a torn and tattered suit, two sizes too large.

Sometimes its hard to tell whether a stray girl is a stray or someone that actually has a home but doesn't want to be there. There may be extenuating circumstances, anything from dead love, to abusive lovers, to habits she may be trying to hide or quit. She may not want to go home because she's trying to extract herself from the situation. These types of girls are not necessarily strays. Most are staying with friends or relatives while they work out their personal situations and this alibi detracts from the general fact that everyone you meet is a stray. Still it's fair to say that most of them are looking for a new home.

Anyway you slice it, strays almost always spell trouble and its almost impossible to tell whose a stray and whose not. It would be nice to find a woman that wasn't running away from someone or something. Who was comfortable in her own skin and could manage her own poisons. However these women were so few and far between they could almost be deemed a mythical creature. If you don't take a chance on a stray every now and then you're guaranteed to end up alone. So think about it, what would you rather do; take your chances on a stray or end up alone?

With some common sense and a little luck, a stray girl might be the best thing that has ever happened to you. Either way you can count on them to be damaged. But then so are you. Don't worry about the sex right off the bat. Be satisfied if they can make a good sandwich. In time you will learn if they are truly meant for you and then you can become lovers. I think the best advise would be go slow. Get to know your chosen stray by spending time with her before jumping into bed. See how the relationship goes in public before moving into a more private setting. They may never become lovers but prove to be new friends, or the relationship may die on the vine. So take your time because only time will tell, and in these situations time is always on your side.

Chapter 96

I don't generally pick up strays. I live a complicated life and heroin addiction is a full time job. I didn't have the time, energy or money to get mixed up in other people's problems. But this girl was different and lord how I could use different. Perhaps I saw some of myself in her. She seemed to be a cut above her chosen environment. I don't know why but for some reason I felt the need to reach out to her in a very direct manner. So I chose the bar stool next to her and ordered a beer and a shot of vodka. I then turned to her and said; "Hi, my name is Steve. Don't panic. I am not a cop. I'm not here to screw with you. I couldn't help but notice you sitting back here in the dark. You don't look well and your problem is obvious to me. I know what you need. I know what you're going through. You're sick. Not regular sick like regular people. You need a fix, now. It's going to get a lot worse before it gets better. Pretty soon your withdrawal will be unbearable. That bourbon is not going to help. When was your last fix?"

"Okay... My name is Susie. What makes you think I need a fix?"

"Because; heroin's what I do. I know junk inside and out and I know what heroin sick looks like. I have been there so I know what it feels like. I can tell you're in the middle of a serious withdrawal. I can help you if you'll let me. All you have to do is trust me. Got any plans for fixing yourself tonight? Are you prepared to spend the next couple of weeks suffering through the pain and sickness of withdrawal."

"I hadn't thought that far ahead. I lost my connection a couple days ago and I've been pretty sick ever since. I can't find any on my own. I've got a little but I don't have a syringe and

I've never fixed a shot."

I spun our bar stools around so that we were facing each other with her legs between mine. I raised my shot glass, touched hers and said; "Then today's your lucky day. I can't stand to watch you suffer and its only going to get worse if you don't get a fix. So come on. Let me help you. You can trust me."

"Okay... I could really use that... but no tricks... no funny business."

"Not to worry."

I drained hit my shot, drank a good half of my beer, threw a ten on the bar and we left. I led her to my truck and she climbed in on the passenger side while I settled behind the steering wheel. I pulled one of my prepared rigs from its hiding place and she watched as I used my cigarette lighter to slowly liquefy it. "This is top of the line stuff. Its some of the best I've ever shot. I don't want to kill you so let's just do half to start. You can always do the other half later. Do you need help or can you get yourself off."

Susie was accepting everything I said as the truth but she couldn't work the rig. "Can you do it for me? I've never got myself off. It's dark and I'm shaking so bad."

So I turned the overhead light on and I showed her where to hold her arm to create a tourniquet. When our chosen vein stood up I gently slid the needle in, pulled back on the plunger and slowly pushed half of the rig into her. She shuttered and gagged, then slumped forward in the seat. I had fixed that shot for me not someone fifty pounds lighter and suddenly I was afraid that even a quarter of a rig might be to much. She gagged and covered her mouth.

However, she held her the own and after the initial surge she relaxed. I pulled the rig from her arm, capped it and watched as she nodded in and out for the next two hours. She was beautiful but tarnished. She could reclaim her beauty if she got off the junk but female junkies stand no better chance getting clean than their male counterparts. What would cause a girl this pretty to get involved with heroin. She seemed out of her depth. She was still very high but as her buzz hit the three hour mark she was able to talk. She looked at me, grinned faintly and said: "Wow... that was good. Do you live around here?"

"Yeah... Dutch Village."

"Let's go to your place. I've got a little money. I can buy us some beer. "

Chapter 97

    I led the way to Dutch Village, skipped stopping for beer, and wove my way through its many buildings and parking lots until I came to mine. Susie followed me into what was a very barren apartment. I had grown use to the lack of furniture but to others it probably looked odd and Susie had offhandedly said; "Where's all your stuff?"

    "I sold everything but the kitchen table and the bed for drug money."

    "Yeah... I know how that goes..."

    She then pulled a small tinfoil packet from her purse and handed it to me. "This is all I've got but you can have it. Maybe we can split it." I said "alright" as I sat down on my side of the bed.

    I set my plate on the bed and opened her pack. It held about one-third of a square. My spoon had a little in it so I had added hers, then drew a little vodka into a rig, lit my candle and washed the sides of my spoon. I then drew a little water into my syringe and used my plunger to crush the heroin while the water boiled. Susie watched me working from the doorway but curiosity finally got the better of her and she came in and sat down on the other side of the bed.

    I was good at prepping dope and watching me seemed to relax her. It was like she had found the guy who was going to take care of her for the foreseeable future. Maybe she had. When I looked at her I got the feeling she was going to be around for a while. Maybe I should warn her of the curse. She could be its third victim. I took the rig from her first shot, liquefied what was left and added a little from what I had just made. I had her sit back against the pillars so she would be comfortable and motioned for her to hold her arm. I gently slid the needle and slowly pushed the entire load into her arm. I looked up to see that she was looking at me and for a second we looked into each others eyes.

She closed her eyes and faintly smiled as heroin sent her sailing into drug induced serenity. I fixed my own shot, blew out the candle, I settled onto the bed beside her. I had a lot of questions about Susie. How could someone this pretty end up shooting heroin? Who got her started? Who got her off? Had some boyfriend got her started then found her habit to expensive and kicked her out forcing her to fend for herself? Had her family turned their back on her because of heroin? Did her friends know? What about the connection she said she had lost? Was that her boyfriend? Did heroin ruin their relationship?

Chapter 98

I woke up around five the next morning to find that Susie was already awake. Sunlight filtered through the window highlighting her blonde hair and giving her an almost angelic glow. I turned on the bedside lamp which added more light to the room. We were about the same age and she was pretty, no doubt about it. But the heroin didn't agree with her and being an addict was hard on her. I could tell that if she hadn't been in a heroin propelled tailspin she would have been a lot prettier. But what struck me was something far different than any mark of beauty. I recognized it immediately. The whites of her eyes were yellow. I took her hand in mine and saw that her fingernails were also yellow. She was Jaundice. Someone had fixed her with dirty needles and now she was very sick.

When she saw the look on my face she asked; "what's wrong?"

I replied "Susie you're sick. Your liver is damaged. Didn't you think something was wrong when your eyes started turning yellow. You should be in the hospital right now and after you take a shower that's exactly where I'm taking you. Somebody has used dirty needles on you. You need to be in a hospital. I don't mean to scare you but this is serious. You need treatment right away."

She said "okay" with a bit of hesitation but I had said all the right things and she seemed to trust me. We had only known each other for about ten hours but Susie was tired and scared and ready to turn control of her life over to someone who knew more about the poison that had been thrust upon her than she did. There was an urgency in my voice and she responded. I guided her to the bathroom and found her a clean towel and washcloth. While she showered, I changed into fresh clothes and prepared three, one-third rigs just in case I stayed at the hospital. When she finally emerged from the bathroom she was wrapped in a towel and crying. "My eyes are yellow... what's happening to me?"

"You've got what they call Jaundice. You're turning yellow because you're liver is not working properly and toxins are building up in your system. If you don't get into a hospital and get the proper treatment you'll die of liver failure."

I stood up and took her into my arms. She was small and frail. Trembling and scared. I held her tight until she relaxed and then I said; "Don't worry." It's not as bad as it can get. With the proper treatment you'll recover. But you've got to go to the hospital. Today. But don't worry. If you want me to, I'll stay with you. I'll make sure you're never alone. Let's do a hit before leaving. One more won't kill you. It will help get you through the process. We'll let the doctors know that you're addicted to heroin and they'll start you on Methadone. That will take care of any withdrawing. You'll be heroin free before you know it. I don't know how long it will take to fix your liver."

I cooked up enough heroin to prepare two rigs, a third for her, a half for me. I got us off and once Susie had settled into her buzz she called her office to tell her boss that she was having a medical emergency. She said she was sick but didn't know exactly what was wrong. She was going to the hospital and she would let him know as soon as she could. I wrapped my to-go rigs in a paper towel and dropped them into the side pocket of my cargo pants. They would get me through the day if she wanted me to stay with her and I had every intention of staying.

We went in through the emergency room door. I found an orderly and told him I needed the receiving physician. I explained to him that I had just met her, I knew she was addicted to heroin and it looked like she was Jaundice. He took one look at her and agreed. After the appropriate paperwork had been completed they assigned her a room and started treating her liver with antibiotics. They also confirmed that heroin was in her system and started her on Methadone to treat her addiction.

Chapter 99

Susie turned out to be a lot sicker than I thought and the regiment her doctors called for had her in the hospital for eight weeks. Once settled in her room she called her employer to let him know that was in the hospital for a liver disorder. She told him that the doctors believed she would be as good as new in a couple weeks. To keep her spirits high I lavished her with gifts. Flowers, books, candy, balloons, a nice bathrobe with matching pajamas and slippers, a C.D. player and C.D.s of her favorite music. I brought her my favorite Moody Blues t-shirt and went by her apartment for a list of things to make her more comfortable. I showed her how to select pay-per-view movies and paid for the movies she watched.

Despite being very sick Susie turned out to be a happy camper. Every week her co-workers would stop by and I tried to give them all the room they needed. But Susie wanted me there with her. She wanted them to know that I was her boyfriend. For me these visits were pure hell. There were too many people in the room at one time. But I remained cool until the last one had left and then I would go into the bathroom and get off.

It may have been intrigue, maybe infatuation. Call it anything you like. Whatever it was it drew me and Susie together and I stayed with her every day, around the clock. The primary effect this had on me was that it drew me out into the public. Out of the darkness of my personal opium den and this had slowed my use dramatically. I went from six hits a day down to three and then two. Susie's liver treatment was a two month ordeal and it included numerous intravenous drugs, multiple blood samples taken several times a day and of course Methadone.

The administered drugs were not that bad but the daily blood drawings were very painful and left her in tears. It made me mad but there was little I could do. I would hold her hand as they drew the blood and she would bury her nails into the palm of my hand. Tears poured down her cheeks and once they were done I would climb into bed with her and hold her tight until her sobbing turned to sniffles. I kissed her neck and promised that I would take care of it just as soon as her doctors made his rounds.

When he showed up I asked him about Susie's daily blood work. They were hurting her and I wanted them to stop. She was responding well to treatment and the doctors believed that she would soon be healthy enough to go home. She was putting on weight but she was still very weak. I believed blood drawn twice daily was overkill and he said that he would check on it and see if he could reduce them.

I could tell that Susie loved the way I defended her. I was her knight in shining armor. We had long talks, shared our painful pasts and as a result the best of Susie came shining through. She was cleaver and had a wonderful sense of humor, which got better as her health improved. To help her regain her strength we started walking the sixth floor corridor. Sometimes we would ride the elevators or sneak to other floors to look around. Apparently a hospital gown and a I.V., pole was all you needed to access almost any part of the hospital. Sometimes I put her in a wheelchair and took her outside or down to the cafeteria for any meal she liked.

I studied her carefully. Despite being sick she was absolutely radiant. Her long blonde hair and green eyes drew the attention of every man who saw her. I didn't care. Let them look. She was with me. You couldn't break us up if you tried. I don't think Susie was even aware of the attention she attracted. If she was she ignored it.

But she tired easily so once our excursion had drained her of energy I would push her back to her room, get her back in bed and while she napped I would knock off one of my rigs and doze along with her. The hospital did an excellent job of caring for her, but her arms were my concern. She was tiny and the daily needles were torturing her. I confronted her doctor a second time and then pulled my chair around so that I was facing her and was aimlessly leafing through a magazine when the evening nurse came by.

"Are you ready for some good news? We're reducing your blood test to once a week. We'll keep you a couple more weeks to sure you're strong enough to go home." Once released she'll need three months of follow up blood work. You'll bring her here once a week and we'll draw her blood. That's the way its got to be. She'll also be on a prescription antibiotics for several more months. Weekly blood work is the only way we can be sure that the antibiotics are working."

Chapter 100

The next two weeks crawled by. Susie had to stay in the hospital to insure she got enough antibiotics. They reduced their blood test to once a day and then once a week. A turning point in our relationship came one afternoon when Susie caught me smiling at her and asked me "what I was grinning about?" I thought about it for a second and then answered her back as simply as I could; "I'm watching you sleep and think I'm falling in love with you. I've been alone so long and you make me feel at home. You are so beautiful. The hospital says you're almost healed and I can tell. You're absolutely radiant. I'm using less and less heroin and that's because of you. I'm so happy when we're together and I always want to be with you. I don't know what I'll do if I can't be with you everyday."

Susie was grinning; "I was hoping this subject would come up. When I get out of the hospital I want us to live together. My place, your place, a new place, I don't care. I want to be with you. It doesn't matter where we're at as long as we're together. I don't want to be without you, not even for a night. I love the way you take care of me. The way you defend me. I want to come home to you and I want to sleep in your arms, every night for the rest of my life."

We spent every hour of Susie's last week in the hospital talking about living together. About the things we needed to do to make it happen and what the rewards would be. There were a number of apartment complexes available to us but the one I lived in proved the best. They were close to several nice places to eat and shop. They were also close to the office Susie worked at as well as her old apartment. The hospital had done a great job bringing Susie back to perfect health and after eight weeks she had been released with a prescription for more antibiotics and a stern warning about shooting drugs.

The hospital was not there to resurrect junkies or heal their life threatening illnesses, even if they did have insurance. Susie had taken it all to heart. From her perspective I had saved her life and now she was going to save mine. She didn't want to shot heroin and she didn't want me shooting it either. We had fell in love while she was in the hospital. Two month's was all it took to create a relationship we both considered sacred.

We were a perfect fit and neither us seemed ready to push the "heroin" issue. If you had asked we both would have said that we were meant to be together. Maybe we needed each other. Maybe we were just afraid to be alone. Being a junkie can be a lonely life and quitting on you're own is nearly impossible. I had chose to stay with her day and night for the last eight weeks and we had shared major pieces of our life's story. Now I was down to two, one quarter of a rig, hits a day. This reminded me of my earliest days of heroin use and Susie was responsible for this reduction. She was quite the distraction.

Chapter 101

  Along the way we talked about it and I had explained to Susie that I knew I was going to have to stop shooting heroin sometime. I had been lucky and I knew I couldn't be lucky forever, but I wasn't ready to stop just yet. I hadn't stopped while she was in the hospital. I had slowed down and that was a good thing. But I had faithfully brought a couple rigs to the hospital each day and she knew this. There were times when I left the hospital just to keep the heroin train on its tracks. Stepping in at this point would have been a destructive thing to do and I think she knew it. But our relationship was developing and there would come a time when the only issue left unspoken would be heroin.

  Even before leaving the hospital we decided to move her into my apartment. Two weeks after leaving the hospital Susie went back to work. She was still weak and on antibiotics but as the weeks passed she grew stronger. She was a good cook and that had helped us both gain some much needed weight. We spent a lot of time in bed loving on each other. We both seemed starved for affection and preferred being in bed to anything else. We loved making love. We loved to snuggle. To touch. To curl up in a ball and sleep. Susie wanted my arms around her all night long, holding her. The tighter the better.

  She loved saying "I love you." And she wanted to hear it back. If she didn't she would roll over and look me dead in the eye. Sometimes I would play possum to tease her but the longer she studied my face the harder it was to ignore her. Eventually I would grin and she would laugh. We would then melt into each other and make love again. Because of the love Susie and I shared I forgot Diane. As our love grew Melinda slipped away and pretty soon Susie was the only woman on my mind. I did love her but I was slow to say those words.

Chapter 102

We would often shower together as a prelude to making love and we would always drain the water heater. While in the shower Susie would look at my arms and spend time gently washing them. There was no doubting the fact that she wanted me off smack and every time she brought up the subject she grew more and more persistent. I had been lucky and without heroin I could get a job and we could enjoy a healthy life. We could leave the past behind and start anew.

I had listened to her and agreed with most of it. But I didn't quit. I slowed my use and this had helped me in a number of ways. First, I held on to my stash so I didn't have to spend money on heroin. Second, the health of my arms and ankles improved dramatically because I wasn't shooting as much and my loads were small. Third, I didn't want to lose Susie because she had became, by far, the most important, positive part of my life. When she stopped using heroin she literally blossomed.

She recovered from a potentiality deadly round of Jaundice and was now a beautiful young lady with long blonde hair, gorgeous green eyes and a body built for sin. Her arms bore no signs of intravenous drug use and her liver had healed perfectly. One of the things I found most interesting about Susie was her willingness to swap war-stories. She was not ashamed of her encounter with heroin. Her boyfriend had got her hooked and then left her. He had been buying all their smack and getting her off so when he disappeared she didn't know what to do. I had came along just in time.

One thing she said really struck me. She had been in a very suicidal state of mind the night we met. If I had not went to that bar, or ignored her when I got there, she would have probably committed suicide just to get away from the sickness of withdrawal. From her perspective I was heaven sent. If I had not came into her life that night we would have never met. I believed her. I knew that heroin sick was so bad you would prefer death over life. But life takes strength and determination to live it courageously.

Heroin was unnatural. Nothing should be able to make you feel that good. We had both lived through heroin addition and we were proud survivors. When it became my turn I spilled my guts. I told her everything. From my original drug encounter, to the deaths of Melinda and Diane. I had experienced the pleasure of knowing two beautiful, intelligent women and suffered incredible, heart break following their deaths. To think that God's master plan had been to teach me how to appreciate the beauty of a woman and treasure their complexity by killing these two women was beyond ironic. It was cruel.

But the truth was if our individual lives had not taken the routes they had, for better or worse, Susie and I would have never met. These conversations would have never happened and we would never have enjoyed the simply pleasure of washing dishes together. I may have initiated our relationship and for that Susie would be forever grateful, but she was looking at the big picture and she wanted us to be healthy, wealthy and wise. That was the only way we would make it in the long run.

Shooting heroin was a stupid waste of time and money and the health risk was just too great. If I had made it to this point and not died from an overdose or destroyed my liver I needed to thank my lucky stars and look at our relationship as a second chance at a good life. Get a job, go to church, make some thing of our lives. Get married, buy a house, maybe have a couple of kids. We were in charge of our lives and we needed to use this second opportunity to leave the world of drugs behind.

Chapter 103

Once finished with the dishes we stood at the sink holding each other. We were a perfect fit in more ways than one and for the first time in our relationship I said, "I love you." Susie pulled away, stood up on her tip-toes, looked me in the eye and with an air of extreme importance, simply said; "You better." I then went in to the bedroom, prepared a small shot and fed the monster. Ten minutes later I joined her on the couch. In the past that load would have sent me to the Moon.

Now I was using just enough to get by. I was weaning myself off heroin. The professionals will tell you that you have to do it for yourself but truthfully I was doing it for Susie. I was beginning to dread the needle and the smell of cooking tar made me gag. The golden eye was losing and I loved the fact that Susie was winning. I would soon be heroin free and I had to admit that I was ready for this death match to be over. We treasured the relationship we had forged out of thin air and when I looked into her eyes I saw my future. Those spiritual pools of mercurial green held visions of good things to come.

For the first time in five years I was involved in a solid, dependable home based relationship. Susie and I were committed to one another. It was love and faith, trust and dedication. So, when she went back to work I cleaned myself up, bought some new clothes and started looking for a job. I needed to work as much for her as for myself. I was pretty sure she wouldn't stick around if I didn't get a job. A second job would bring in some much needed cash and allow us to have some clean, healthy fun. But for me a new job was easier said than done.

Despite having paperwork which stated I had been laid-off for no fault of my own and a personal letter of recommendation from my Divisional Manager I couldn't find a descent job. I lost the opportunities that required a drug test. I was always hot and failed every drug test I took. It got to the point that when they gave me instructions to take a drug test I just walked away from the opportunity. Susie used this issue to point out my drug problem and of course I had to agree.

I started looking for work in the retail sector but had no luck. It was very discouraging. But I didn't give up. I worked every led, enlisted the help of the Employment Security Commission and registered with temporary agencies. It was through one of the temp services that I got my first break. It was a long term construction job and while I wasn't interested in construction, Susie said it was a start and that I should take advantage of it. I could always trade up as other opportunities presented themselves.

So I took the job and I tried to do it. But I was not cut out for hard, manual labor. Years of heroin abuse had left me weak and they wanted me on the job at 6 AM which was simply impossible. So I went back to the temp agency looking for anything indoors. Entry level retail, warehouse; anything inside. I also talked to the ESC about my benefits and because I was using them to help me find a job they approved a six week extension. Susie had taken it all in stride and refused to let me get discouraged. Something good was going to happen. It was just taking a little longer than usual.

I loved her more for believing that than anything else. She was not giving up on me. She had faith in me. She saw something in me that I had lost when I started using heroin again. As you might expect I was not a happy camper. Job hunting was depressing work and with each rejection came the desire to use more and more heroin. It quickly became a tug a war between what I knew was right and heroin. I didn't want to lose Susie, I wanted to work, but with each passing job interview and with absolutely no calls for a second interview my spirit sank pretty low.

Chapter 104

Then came a particularly depressing week. There were no ads in the Sunday paper that even remotely applied to me and I couldn't think of a single establishment to apply for work at. I called the temporary agencies but they had nothing new. There was nothing I could do. There was nowhere to go. Susie had said not to worry about it. We had money in the bank, a roof over our head and food in the refrigerator. Something was sure to come along and I could spend the day cleaning house. I felt totally dejected.

Susie then went to work leaving me and the monster at home alone. Neither of us could have imaged what my mind would do next. But on this particular day, when left to my own devices, I went fucking crazy. A voice from nowhere resonated in my brain asking; "How much smack do you think you can do at one time?" I knew this was the golden eye; the voice of junk. The eye had been content to let me build a relationship with Susie but now it was back to claim what belonged to it.

After years of letting me destroy myself. Of hedging me into solitary confinement. Of taking me to the edge of heroin induced death and forcing me to find my own way back. Of simply not letting me die. Of letting me walk this earth in a hell of my own making and refusing me the peace of death. The eye had came to claim my soul. For the first time in my junkie life, the golden eye had competition and I think it came after me that morning because it knew if it didn't, it would never get another chance.

I loved Susie beyond measure. Our hearts beat as one and our spirits were entwined. We were in each others head. Always knew what the other was thinking. Could even finish each others sentences. When you're that in love it's a wonderful place to be. But I had a devilish thirst for heroin and this morning, with the golden eye in my head, that thirst would not be denied.

Suddenly, it was almost as if my movements were being controlled by a force outside my body. I found a huge spoon and set myself to preparing everything would I need to shoot the most heroin I had ever shot at one time. I went through the steps required to pack one rig with junk so thick the plunger would barely push it. Then, for the first time in a year and for the last time in my life I used my left arm to get off. Its veins were either collapsed or callused so that it took a minute to find a usable vein.

It wasn't easy. I worked slow and steady. I was a pro and I had learned a few tricks along the way. I used a garrote instead of a tourniquet so it could be released by just letting go. I then took a piece of duct tape, about six inches long, slid the needle into my chosen vein and taped the rig to my arm. I made sure the needle didn't come out of its vein and then slowly pushed the entire load into my arm. I released the garrote and the junk exploded in my brain. It was like dynamite, like being hit with a bat, like being run over by a train. Pick your heroin euphemism.

This time I chose death over life and there was no way I would survive. Heroin plowed through my system, blurring my vision and for a moment I thought I was going to vomit. I fought the nausea. I had lived for many years with a needle in my arm. Now I was going to die that way. I gagged. Swallowed. I didn't want to get sick. I didn't want to be found covered in vomit. I leaned forward and rolled off the bed. The last thing I remember was the eyelashes on my right eye brushing the carpet, back and forth, as my reflexes slowed to the point of death.

I was paralyzed. Everything was shutting down. My breathe was changing, becoming shallow and irregular. It felt like a great weight was holding me down while at the same time I was floating away. Heroin pushed me out of my body and my vision floated upward. There was nothing, no thought, no feeling. Heroin pulled a curtain between me and my body. There would be no return. I floated upward and away until I simply evaporated into nothingness. I had became what the golden eye had always wanted. No light, no sound, no voices, no laughter. Just an eerie in and out and a final puff of smoke.

Chapter 105

But Susie had inadvertently saved my life. She had set up an appointment with the maintenance man to work on the garbage disposal and she had left the door open so that he could get into the apartment. He had opened the front door just in time to see me fall over dead. He dialed 911 and then pulled me into the living room and began administrating CPR. The ambulance arrived in minutes. When they saw my syringes and spoon they administered multiple injections of Naloxone trying to reverse the heroin's effect. Multiple injections and non-stop CPR brought me back from the dead, however, my body was full of heroin and they had incubated me on the spot.

They had radioed the hospital and told them to be ready for a heroin overdose requiring life support. They continued administering Naloxone however I was in a heroin induced coma and a multitude of machines were used to keep me alive. I spent twenty seven days in that coma. My doctors thought I would die despite the machines, however I defied their expectations.

In my coma I dreamed that the gray man was sitting in a chair beside my bed. It looked like he was covered in a layer of ash and dirt. His eyes were pools of blood and his movements were stiff and rickety. He sat there, hands resting on his knees, head moving slowly from side to side. He focused on me and tried to speak but when he did ashes and dirt poured from his mouth. His movements became more agitated and shook his head from side to side causing blood to flow from his eyes down his face.

He clapped his hands together and an over sized syringe appeared between them. He struggled to his feet, raised the syringe over his head and plunged it into my chest. He pulled back on the plunger and drained my body of all its blood. When he finished I was as gray as he was. His syringe was full of my blood and he staggered back and forth trying to hold it aloft. He swung that bloody syringe wildly trying to maintain his balance before finally falling into a pile of dirt beside my bed.

Even though I was in a coma I experienced this dream as if it was actually happening. It was terrifying and I had responded with unconscious violence. The hospital had to restrain me by tying me to my bed hoping to keep me from tearing out I.V.s that they had worked so hard inserting in to my damaged and abused veins. They assigned a medical assistant to watch me 24/7 to make sure my unconscious actions did not get out of hand. The hospital had no way of knowing what was going on in my head and they were not going to prescribe sedatives to someone in a drug induced coma. So I was left to deal with the insanity unfolding behind my eyes and they were content to keep an eye on the machines.

Chapter 106

When Susie learned what I had done she was devastated. How could I be so self destructive? She was terrified by the thought that I might never wake up and had spent every possible hour at the hospital. On the twenty-seventh day of my coma my doctors starting using small amounts of adrenaline to bring me out of my coma. They had been successful but I was not out of the woods. The violence I expressed while in my coma was nothing compared to the violence I expressed when I came to.

At first hospital staff did not realize I was awake and the only thing going through my crazy brain was; "Their going to steal your organs." I pulled against the gauze holding my right arm in place for a good thirty minutes before freeing myself. I broke my right wrist and elbow in the process but I was a man on a mission. I reached behind me with my right hand and grabbed the monitor pole just to the right of my head. At the same time I sled down the bed as far as I could. I pulled the monitor free and brought it across my body, crashing it into the attendant sitting just beyond my left foot. He never saw it coming.

The incubation tube was the next medical device I tried to remove from my body. Trying to pull this apparatus from my throat was a new experience in pain. My insane mind was screaming for release. If given the time I could have freed myself of every tether no matter the pain but then there were nurses streaming around the curtain, two on each side, injecting me with multiple shoots in each shoulder.

They knocked me out cold and I did not wake up until late the next day. This time I was tied to the bed with leather straps and the incubation tube had been removed. My original attendant had been replaced by an enormous security guard. As I came to and everything slowly came into focus I saw him standing there. When he saw that I was looking at him he pointed at his eyes, then mine and finally he pulled on the leather straps. His message was clear. I wasn't going anywhere.

Chapter 107

Once conscious, my doctors determined that I had contracted pneumonia breathing the hospital's air and I was moved from ICU to the eighth floor for further treatment. Trying to tear out the incubation tube had left my throat in a very ragged condition so there was a treatment plan in place to address this. The next time Susie came to the hospital I was awake and mildly sedated. Nodding in and out. Neither conscious nor unconscious. I had I.V.s in both arms, an air tube feeding me oxygen, my arms were being treated for infection with antibiotic ointment and bandages. I had also broke my right wrist and elbow so these breaks were in cast.

When Susie saw me sitting up she broke into a giant grin and began clapping, laughing and crying at the same time. She was mad, relieved and happy. She started punching my shoulder with her ineffectual fists and wore herself out with questions: "How could I do that? Didn't I love her? Why would I do that? What was I thinking? Didn't I care about our relationship? Didn't I want to be with her? Didn't I want us to be together."

I left the "voices in my head" part out and told her that with no job interviews for the day I had decided to enjoy heroin all day and be returned to normal by the time she got home from work. I told her I had just done too much at one time. None of this changed the fact that I loved her or wanted to be with her. I couldn't imagine life without her and I was sorry for acting selfish.

"Well...okay. I believe you. I know you love me. I can feel it. I love you. I thought I lost you. I've been talking to your doctors and they want you to go to a ninety day rehab program as soon as you can. The only chance we have at being together is if you stop using heroin. If you can't stop I can't be with you. I won't let you drag me down. I'm not going back to that lifestyle. Now you've got to make a choice. It's either me or heroin. Look at me. What man in his right mind would choose heroin over this?"

She ran her hands up and down her curvy body, across her flat stomach, around her ample breast and up her neck into her hair. She shook her hair out then slowly turned one continuous circle that brought her back to looking at me.

"Okay, okay, I get it. I choose you."

"You'd be stupid not to. Look at me. On a scale of one to ten I'm at least a twelve. On top of that I love you, even after something this stupid. But we're gonna come up with some rules and I want you off heroin, starting now. Do you understand? This is no way to live and I love you so you get one break. But I can do better than a shot-up junkie so you've got some catching up to do."

"I know, you're right. I don't know what I'd do without you. I'm addicted to you and you're sweeter than heroin by a long shot. Thanks to the coma I haven't used heroin in five weeks but I'll need methadone to stop. I don't want to lose you. I love you so much. Smack is so fucked up. It just ruins your life. At first it seems sweet but really its a monster. I didn't mean to drag you through this."

"Well, one good turn deserves another. You saved me so now I'm going to save you."

"I'll get clean while I'm here and I'll go to rehab as soon as they say I'm ready. Will you come see me?"

"Of course I will. Every chance they let me. I love you. I want to be with you. But I want you straight. No more drugs. If you keep going you'll ruin our relationship and kill yourself. I can't stand to watch that happen, so if you don't stop I'll leave and never come back."

"I understand. I don't want to lose you. You're the best

thing in my life. But I've never been sober. I'm a junkie and you know why."

"I know and I hate that for you. But you're with me now. You've got to leave the past behind and focus on our future. You can't obsess over dead people. The past is gone. Get over it. The deaths of Melinda and Diane were tragic events no doubt about it. But I'm here and I'm alive. You'll never find a better woman. Let's put the past behind us and start planning our future."

"Okay. I'll go to rehab and after rehab we'll build a relationship designed to last a lifetime."

"Your doctor said that you would be on Methadone for at least a year, maybe longer. Your treatment to break your addiction started two days ago and everybody understands that it may take a long time. But Methadone will be available as long as you need it. Once you're out of rehab I expect you to stay clean and get a job so that we can start moving forward again."

Chapter 108

Susie then climbed over the railing and lay down beside me on the bed. She held me, kissed me, draped her leg over mine and whispered in my ear; "I have missed you so much. At first your doctors thought you were going to die. But I didn't let myself believe that. I prayed for you everyday, all day long and you came back to me. I'm not surprised. Our love is strong. We're going to live a long, wonderful life. I believe that."

She then lowered her voice to a whisper, leaned in close to my ear and starting saying things I can't repeat, but oh my god, how they got my attention. She was in charge and she knew it. She could have any man she wanted. For some reason she wanted me and for the life of me I can't tell you why.

I didn't tell Susie about the "gray man." He was my latest reoccurring nightmare but I wasn't sure what the dream meant so I said: "I believe that everything good happens to us because of you. I've never told you this but the first night we met you looked like an angel. Something moved inside of me and I have often wondered what force pushed me toward you. But once I saw you I knew I had to save you.

In an instant you became my better half. At that point I didn't even know you were sick. But I knew you were special and being with you would be lie changing. You were worth saving and you're wonderful to be with now. You're like a gift from heaven and I am so lucky to have you in my life."

I looked into her beautiful green, positively hypnotic eyes. I got lost in those eyes and she was smiling because she knew the effect she had on me. Our love was mutual. At this point we would do anything for each other. It was almost like the good times were just beginning. There were things about me that she would never know and there were things about her that she would never tell and if she kept me busy those things would never matter.

She kissed me and said; "I think the same of you. We're each others gift from heaven. Together we'll make it. We're a team. Good, better, best. Never let it rest. Until the good is better and the better is best."

"Where did you hear that?"

"My mother would say it to me everyday when I was a child and as soon as I knew it by heart we would say it together. Everyday. Sometimes two or three times a day. She brainwashed me with that little quote. I say it to myself all the time and I want you to start saying it to yourself."

"Good, better, best. Never let it rest. Until the good is better and the better is best."

Chapter 109

I spent the next three weeks getting over pneumonia and as promised, Methadone settled me down. I started to return to something that resembled me, without heroin. It was so very surreal and each day was a learning experience. I didn't know who I was. It was confusing. I knew how to be a heroin addict. I knew how to live from shot to shot. I had done that for years. I could cook dope with the best of them. Being sober was confusing. It took away the thing I did best. I found it hard to deal with sober people. I didn't know how to be sober.

Methadone took away the craving but it didn't give you a buzz and that was a problem for me. I loved the danger. I loved the high. I didn't know what to do with myself. I was haunted. I had lost every person I had ever loved and spent seven of the last twelve years addicted to a drug over which I had no control. I was a sober junkie trying to live in a sober world. If asked I would have said; "I don't like it."

But I had promised this gorgeous, green eyed blonde, who loved me despite of my many faults, that I would turn my back on heroin and I would. It was just proving harder than I originally thought. I didn't know how to manage my time. I had to carefully measure my words because I wasn't sure what would come out of my mouth. I couldn't remember large chunks of my past and my future was a blank slate. Susie was the only thing I could set my eyes on.

I made these factors known to the psychiatrist that visited me once a day for an hour or so and she had said that for someone addicted to heroin for as long as I had been, all of this was normal. I could expect this and more as I worked through the stages of rebuilding my life. I had lived through large chunks of my life addicted to heroin. Now I had to live sober or die. I would eventually remember some things, some things I would never remember and some things were worth forgetting. It may take years for me to remember certain things. I would remember something new every day but I didn't need to worry about the past. I needed to worry about the future and that meant I had to commit to sober living.

Chapter 110

As it turns out pneumonia really kicked my ass. I was almost too weak to breath much less walk. Susie used this opportunity to love on me. She took a week of vacation and spent every hour of every day, for nine days straight, in the hospital with me. She brought my favorite Chinese food, had my 24/7 guard take pictures of us in bed together and filled the window sill with flowers. However, for the most part, if she was at the hospital, she was in the bed with me and she didn't care who knew it. I was hers and she was mine.

If they wanted blood or needed to administer some kind of medicine they had to untangle us. Some times we cuddled or slept, sometimes we talked about our future and sometimes we whispered sweet loving into each others ear. She was my only interest and she loved being the center of my attention.

It took some time but I slowly got over pneumonia. Of course I was poked and prodded, drained daily of blood and hooked to various I.V.s. But as days turned into weeks my appetite improved and I started regaining my strength. My attending nurse told me that I had to get out of bed and start walking. The next day an attendant came by to get me started. She showed me how to bring my I.V., pole with me so I could walk the corridor. At first I had to hold the I.V., pole with one hand and the railing that lined the corridor with the other. I was quick to ran out of breath and very weak.

For a good week and a half I could only do one lap but as time went by I got stronger and before long I could make the journey on my own. Then it was just a matter of increasing my laps. I was told that when I could walk the corridor ten times without stopping I would be released and that gave me a goal.

Even though I was still weak I insisted on walking and Susie was eager to help me do it. She would walk with me pushing a wheelchair. When I pushed myself as far as I could go I would collapse into the wheelchair and she would push me back to the room and help me into bed.

As time went by I got stronger and every couple of days my lap count increased. Susie had been with me when I walked ten laps and she had told the nurse I had finally made it. To make sure the nurse came by the next morning and walked with me. We made it around ten times and she recorded my progress in my chart and I was cleared for rehab.

Chapter III

The next day my doctor stopped by to give me a crash course on life at rehab. No fighting, no drugs of any kind and since it was a co-ed facility, no sex of any kind. The program was free if I passed it and incredibly expensive if I didn't. I had to sign a contract that spelled out these rules and they were pretty clear. If I kept my nose clean and made it through the program I would leave with a clean bill of health and I could continue using Methadone as long as I needed it. If I broke the rules I would be kicked out of the program and forced to pay five-hundred dollars a week for each week I had been there.

For some participants, the first week at rehab was spent in detox. For those of us who had already went through detox the first week was spent learning what addiction meant. The counselor made it clear that there was no difference between a junkie and an alcoholic. Either way you were trapped by a substance that was stronger than you and in the end would kill you. The destructive impact of addiction showed itself in every aspect of an addicts life; from their inability to get and keep a job, to their general health and well being, to the way they interacted with family and friends.

Community based organizations such as the church of our choice, Alcoholic's Anonymous, Al-anon and Narcotic's Anonymous would help if you faithfully worked the steps. In the end it all came down to you and free will. You either loved your poison and died, or you walked away from it and lived.

By the end of week three I wanted to see Susie so bad it felt like I was going through withdrawal all over again. But there she was and when the staff saw us waving at each other they let her into the day room. We rushed together and for a good five minutes just stood there holding each other. For the first time in a long time I was sober and in love.

There were benches and swings at various places throughout the gardens and I led her to one of the swings. It was there that I asked Susie to marry me. My proposal was met with an enthusiastic "yes. Let's get our parents together and go from there."

"Cool... I was beginning to wonder if you actually had a family."

"Of course I have a family. But they live in Hawaii. I've been very careful not to let them know what I've been up to the last two years. But with you it's different. I want them to meet you. I want them to know we're getting married and they can expect grandchildren."

She took my hand and pressed it to her stomach. "The doctor says I'm between about ten weeks along. If you trace that back you'll see that I got pregnant sometime between me getting out of the hospital and you're insane overdose. It was like you couldn't get enough of me. You literally chased me around the apartment. If we were at home you wanted me in bed. Want to know a secret? I loved being chased by you. I loved it when you caught me. You made me feel wanted. I let you catch me. You know how to push my buttons. And you never wore a condom. It was like you were trying to get me pregnant."

"Susie, you've got to realize you're like no other woman I've ever known. You're chemistry makes me glow. You're an angel from head to toe. There's something about you that makes my blood boil. I feel for you like I've never felt for anyone. I lust for you, for your taste, your smell. You make me crazy. Your sex drives me out of my mind. I want you all the time. Rehab is killing me because I can't be with you. I sleep good when you're in the bed with me. In here I barely sleep at all."

Chapter 112

We curled up on that swing and I held her all afternoon. We were like pieces of a puzzle that had been brought together to complete our lives. We were two very deserving people. We had both taken some hard hits and we had each spent a fair amount of time in the hospital. But we had found each other and there was no mistaking the love we shared. The first five months of our relationship had been a flash in the pan; a frenzy of drugs and hospital stays, followed by three weeks of unbridled, intoxicating sex.

Now my desire for Susie's sex had turned into a raging demand and so the last few weeks of rehab had been tedious at best. Time slowed to a crawl and with each visit my desire for Susie grew stronger. By the time my release rolled around her sex was all I could think of. Rehab granted me another chance at life. It had reintroduced me to sober living. This was my life after death. This was my clean slate. For better or worse, I knew I would never get another chance. On the day I was released Susie was there to pick me up. There was no ceremony. Just sign a few papers, take my copies and I was free to go.

When I walked out of rehab the world had changed. It was somehow cleaner and brighter. For the first time in three and a half years I was clean and sober and I must admit I didn't like it very much. I wasn't looking through the haze of heroin. I wasn't outside for the sole purpose of scoring heroin. The world was full of possibilities and all of them scared the hell out of me. However, Susie had said we would take things one at a time and neither of us doubted what came first.

We were so hungry for each other that we rented a motel room just outside Greensboro and spent the next two days making love. We were clean and sober and our desire for each other knew no limit. We showered and made love. Dined on room service and made love. Watched T.V., and made love. Slept and made love. We swam in the pool and made love. By the time we left the motel we were exhausted and yet when we got home the first thing we did was make love. We then fell asleep and didn't wake up until the next morning.

Chapter 113

I had been gone from the apartment for almost six months. Hadn't shot heroin in almost six months. Hadn't drank alcohol or smoked a cigarette in almost six months. I didn't realize how out of control my life had been until I looked back at it with sober eyes. I was happy to just be alive. I had gained thirty pounds since overdosing and was healthier now than at any time since returning to North Carolina five years prior. Melinda and Diane's death had hit me hard. Heroin had almost destroyed me.

And then there was Susie. The angel who came from out of nowhere to become the center of my life. I never wanted her out of my sight because I was afraid something might happen and she wouldn't make it back. So I was glad to see that she had used my truck to move a lot of her stuff to my apartment. It actually made me happy and I had said; "You really know how to make this place feel like home."

"It's coming around. You didn't have any furniture so I've been decorating. My stuff looks okay but I thinking about having a yard sale and using the money to buy some better stuff. What do you think?"

"That sounds great. I'm sure the manager won't care if we do the yard sale here. It shouldn't take long to get ready for a yard sale. We'll stage the yard sale to your apartment and then bring it over here."

I didn't have any furniture to speak of so all we were really doing was bringing Susie's furniture to my apartment. Things she didn't want would be sold at the yard sale. Our first Saturday arrived and we went to Susie's apartment, loaded her bedroom furniture into my truck and returned to my apartment. We moved my bedroom furniture onto the patio and set up her bedroom suit. Queen size bed, tables on either side and a chest of drawers. She made the bed with fresh sheets, a comforter and rows of pillows.

We needed to protect my furniture so I pulled around to load my stuff with the idea being to take it to Susie's apartment for storage until we could do the yard sale. When I opened the nightstand drawer to get a good grip I couldn't believe what I saw. Twenty packs of heroin and a bag of syringes.

Now you're probably thinking that at this point in my life I would do the right thing and take them to Susie to show her I was committed to sobriety. But no... instead of doing the right thing, I did what any seasoned junkie would do. I slid the heroin and rigs into the side pocket of my cargo pants. The golden eye was back. Susie had failed to check that drawer and now I had twenty packs of heroin and ten rigs. I now worked in greedy anticipation of reintroducing myself to heroin. My sobriety was over.

*   *   *

Don't give up, it takes awhile
I have seen this look before
And it's alright, you're not alone
If you don't love this anymore

I hear that you slipped again
I'm here 'cause I know you need a friend

And you know that accidents can happen
And it's okay, we all fall off the wagon sometimes
It's not your whole life, it's only one day
You haven't thrown everything away

Take some time, learn to breathe
And remember what it means
To feel alive and to believe
Something more than what you see

I know there's a price for this
But some things in life you must resist

Sixx A.M. The Heroin Diaries: Accidents Can Happen
Darren Jay Ashba, James Michael, Nikki Sixx
Lyrics © Downtown Music Publishing LLC
Warner Chappell Music Inc.
Sixx Gunner Music

Chapter 114

For all that Susie was, and she was incredible in so many ways, the golden eye was always one step ahead of her. It was the devil that never went away. Once you're addicted you're always an addict. Susie and I spent the rest of the day working on our apartment. While she decorated the living room I fired up the grill and cooked hamburgers. With dinner out of the way we took a shared shower during which I paid every inch of her body my complete and undivided attention.

I couldn't keep my hands and mouth off of her. Our shower had lasted until the water ran cold and Susie cried out that she; "couldn't possibility get any cleaner. I'm being molested by my lover. I'm getting out of this shower and going to bed. If you want anymore of me that's where I'll be."

Once in bed we reveled in our love, the sensation of our bodies as we touched. I never grew tired of her playfulness, her tenderness, her kindheartedness. And yes her sexuality. She was the complete package. Her beauty was staggering. From her long blonde hair and beautiful green eyes to her perfect, gorgeous body. She was a centerfold and I knew that I would never know a better woman. We made love to each other slow and gentle, until we were both pleasantly exhausted. We whispered our love to one another.

Considered our love a perfect union and her pregnancy a sacred product of that union. We both knew how precious our love was and what the future held if we focused on what we truly wanted. Sunday came and we made a simple plan. Eat breakfast and then go to Susie's apartment to work on the yard sale. As she priced things I boxed them up and slowly there emerged a stack of yard sale boxes. There were a few things Susie wanted at home so I boxed them up and drove back to our apartment.

I was literally salivating. My mind hallucinated the feel of heroin and I thought long and hard about how I was going to actually do it. I wasn't about to start shooting it but I knew I could make a simple, fairly durable pipe by folding a foot square of aluminum foil into a four inch strip. Wind it around a pen then tape it in place and used the pen's blunt end to create an upturned bowl. I had never tried this with heroin but the junkie in me was doing what it had to do to get a fix.

There were a number of benefits to this way of thinking. One; I could throw the rigs away and put an end to the junkie in me. Two; what I had would last for a longer period of time. Three; If I could stay clean until I got a job I could then leisurely smoke heroin and no one would be the wiser. I liked these points but I knew Susie would never go for any of them. If I didn't stay clean I would never pass a piss test and that would reveal my heroin use. If this happened Susie would be gone.

Chapter 115

Once again I was in a bind of my own making. Smoking heroin was better than shooting it. But that was still doing it and eventually it would show up in the same old ways. In the best of all worlds I would get a job before I got hot and that would keep Susie from knowing I had heroin. But heroin made finding a job impossible. Despite my simple job requirements I knew I would test hot and never be offered a second interview no matter how insignificant the job might be. This was was a no win situation and I had returned to Susie with no solution in place.

When I got there she said she was hungry and wanted something to eat. So I got a meal plan together and headed for a local restaurant. But first I stopped by the apartment to build my idea of a heroin pipe. Multiple layers of aluminum foil, folded into a strip four inches wide, rolled into a nice tight cylinder and bent upward on one end to form a bowl. I taped it together, broke off a piece of heroin, packed it into the bowl and used my lighter to start cooking it. It boiled in the bowl and filled my lungs with smoke. I exhaled and hit it again. I could feel myself getting high and I knew I had to be careful.

If Susie knew this she would leave, it was just that simple. I could not start looking like I was on drugs. So I smoked one more bowl, dropped my pipe into my side pocket and headed out for burgers, fries, Cokes and apple pies. This won't satisfy Susie's hunger for long but it would get us through the next few hours after which I would feed her whatever she wanted. When I got to the apartment I found her sitting on the floor in the middle of a pile of stuff. She was pricing items and when she saw me she broke into a big grin and started clapping. It was this kind of response that made her so beautiful.

"You sound hungry."

"I am hungry. I'm also happy to see you. Give me some sugar."

I laughed and kissed her, slowly and passionately and then looking into her eyes I said; "You are so beautiful. Being hooked on you is doable. I never thought I'd grow old. I always saw myself dying young, but now I have you and you change everything." I knelt beside her and we slowly laid down on the floor, intertwined and kissing. We were so possessed by each other that we could never be together long before ending up in a lover's knot; "I love you so much. I don't think I could live without you. You're so damn sexy. I'll bet you're juicy right now."

"I love the way you talk to me. I get wet just listening to you. You know how to turn me on. I think I could cum just listening to you talk. I want to feel you inside of me. Come on; fuck me. There's nobody here but us. Take my clothes off. Get me naked."

"How about this. Let's eat while it's hot and then we'll go to our apartment. I'll undress your gorgeous body and make love to you all afternoon. I'll make you cum, over and over, until you're exhausted."

Susie face was flushed with desire and her eyes glazed over as she thought about that kind of evening. "Yeah," She whispered, "Let's do that. I'm so horny. I need the attention. Does that sound selfish?"

"I'll do anything you ask. I love you. I want you satisfied. Satisfying you satisfies me, so no you don't sound selfish. You know how to ask for what you want and I want to fulfill you're every desire."

I felt my pipe and rigs dig into my leg and was immediately aware of my dishonesty. I should throw the heroin away. Make the last six months count for something. She was investing everything in our love and throwing the heroin away would keep me honest. Unfortunately honesty was not my style. I loved the high. It was my greatest fault and my supreme weak-ness. Knowing I had heroin was a thrill. That made the golden eye a permanent guest in my house. It was hard to argue with my track record. I had spent seven years addicted to heroin and had been prepared to die for a long time. Nobody in their right mind would have bet on me. But Susie had and it was up to me to make her bet a smart one.

Chapter 116

We ate and talked about our plan for the yard sale. I reminded her that she was pregnant and we were going home once we finished eating. It had already been a successful day. I could work on yard sale stuff through the week and she didn't have to worry about a thing. I would get everything ready to go and would put up fliers Thursday and Friday announcing the sale Saturday between 6 AM and 4 PM. We were close to done so I focused Susie on going home and taking a nap.

"You've got to keep up your strength and you need to go to bed early so that you feel rested in the morning. I need to job hunt next week which means the only deadline we have is being out of this apartment by the end of the month."

So that's what we did. Once back at the apartment I guided Susie to bed and peeled back the covers. I then slowly undressed her, one article of clothing at a time until she stood before me completely naked. I knelt before her kissing her belly, her thighs and her beautiful pussy. I then guided her gently into bed and watched as she stretched out and got comfortable. Her body was simply amazing. I never ceased to be amazed by how sexy she truly was. She was a gorgeous, exquisite goddess, beautiful from head to toe. I kissed her belly, moved slowly to her breast, then her neck and finally her mouth. She purred and spread her legs as I let my fingers retrace the path my kisses had taken. We looked into each others eyes and smiled. Our love was monumental. "Go to sleep beautiful. I'll be here when you wake up."

I watched her drift off and closed the bedroom door behind me. I had promised her an afternoon of sex and I had every intention of making good on that promise. Maybe this afternoon, maybe tomorrow. The war in my mind between her and the golden eye flared up as soon as I did and with Susie on my mind I decided to throw the rigs away. To make sure this happened I got in my truck, drove up to the dumpster and threw them in. This left me with eighteen packs of heroin and one homemade pipe. By throwing the rigs away I had deprived the golden eye of its primary delivery system.

Chapter 117

Score one for Susie. This would make sure I did not return to the life of a junkie. Susie didn't know I was fighting for us and by throwing the rigs away I had won one for the home team. I then went to the grocery store and bought the foods I knew Susie liked. Pickles, ice cream, potato chips, chocolate chip cookies, bananas, strawberries, whipped cream and Sprite. I then bought fifty dollars worth of Chinese food. By five-thirty I was putting groceries away and setting the table. I then opened the bedroom door and found Susie half awake. I sat down on the bed and took her hand in mine. After a few minutes she yawned, stretched and looked up at me smiling. I smiled back and gently caressed her belly. I kissed her hand, her nipples, her neck, her earlobes and finally her mouth. I looked into those incredible green eyes and asked; "Did you have a good nap?"

"I had a wonderful nap. You're making me horny."

"Let's eat first. Then we'll take care of horny. Want to eat in bed, at the kitchen table or on the couch?"

"On the couch."

"Okay... Are you ready to get up?"

"Yes... boy I slept hard. I feel worn out."

"Your pregnant. We've got to compensate for that. I'm going to take care of you every day, every meal."

"I like the sound of that. You take great care of me now."

I tossed her my favorite Moody Blues t-shirt, the one I bought when I saw their concert with Melinda back in the mid '80s and which she had wore every night since I had brought it to her in the hospital. As she moved from the bed to the couch I fixed her a large plate of Chinese food and a large Sprite. When she finished that one I fixed her another one and when she finished that one I made her an ice cream Sunday. I gave her a handful of fortune cookies and listened as she read the best ones out loud: "People learn little from success, but much from failure." Another said; "Life's many pleasures await you" while another read; "When you approach life's crossroads, look both ways."

Chapter 118

While Susie busied herself with fortune cookies I cleaned up the kitchen. I closed the food boxes and put them in the refrigerator. I put the ice cream in the freezer and threw everything else in the trash. I washed the dishes and put them away. When I returned to the living room Susie had stretched out on the couch and was watching T.V. I sat down on the opposite end of the couch, took her feet in my lap and began massaging them. "Oh... that feels so good" she purred, tensing her feet and spreading her toes. She relaxed into the attention, closed her eyes and drifted off to sleep.

I let an hour go by and then I picked her up and carried her to bed. She relaxed into the bedding and I stepped out on the patio for a cigarette. I ended up smoking heroin for the next forty-five minutes. I needed sleep. Without it I would soon be in big trouble. I quietly went back inside, stripped to my boxers and slipped into bed. I pulled Susie to me and drifted off to sleep. It had been an interesting day. Susie was happy and for me that was the most important thing. I was not going to let heroin come between us. Sure, I was going to smoke what I had and probably buy more. But there was no rush.

Susie would win. Right now, at that moment, I was holding the most important thing in my life in my arms, and she was sleeping safe and sound. The next morning I woke up before she did and fixed her a massive breakfast hoping that a more food at different times during the day would help with her energy levels. When everything was on the table I went into the bedroom and found Susie awake but still in bed. I kissed her forehead, cheek and mouth. In response she smiled and stretched; "Man I slept good."

"I know. You must have been really tired because you barely moved all night."

"I woke up a few times but each time I was in your arms so I just went back to sleep."

"Well it's time for you to get up. Breakfast is on the table and you've got to get ready for work."

I retrieved her bathrobe and Susie slipped out of my t-shirt into her robe. We settled at the kitchen table and I loaded her plate with some of everything. I fixed myself a cup of coffee and asked her about her next doctor's appointment. "First thing Wednesday morning. Want to go with me?"

"I'd love to. I'll drive you there and then take you to work. I'll go grocery shopping, spend some time packing yard sale items and bring you a good lunch. After lunch I'll take you back to work and then I'll come back for you at five-thirty."

As Susie cleaned portions of her plate I reloaded it. I reminded her that she was eating for two and that was all it took to get her to eat a second helping of everything. Finally she pushed away from the table and said; "I'm stuffed. I can't eat another bite."

"Okay... I'll clean this up while you take a shower. Get a move on. You don't need to be late."

"What are you going to do today?"

"I'm going to get a Sunday paper and try to find some job leads."

She kissed me and said, "good for you and thank you for breakfast. I love the way you're taking care of me. To think that when I found out I was pregnant I was worried about telling you. Boy was I wrong."

"So how far along do you think you are?"

"Around four months, give or take."

"Time is flying. I don't see how we can possibly get married and go to Hawaii before your due date. Maybe we should focus on a small wedding and try to see your parents after the baby is born. I know that's not you're first choice but we've got to be realistic. I'd rather spend the money on an

259

engagement ring and a set of wedding bands instead of airline tickets to Hawaii. That way you would look properly engaged and officially married."

"An engagement ring with a wedding band? Yeah... I like the sound of that."

"It makes our relationship official. I think we should take care of that this week. Maybe we can go ring shopping one afternoon or maybe I'll just surprise you."

"I've never had an engagement ring. So yeah. Let's do that. Then we'll focus on meeting your parents. I'll call mine and feel them out for how we can get together. What about your parents?"

"I'll call them today and we can have lunch with them this coming Sunday. My sisters will love you and since nobody knows about what I've been doing lately we can look all sweet and innocent."

"And in love, don't forget that. Plus we can meet them before I start showing. I was really hoping you could meet my parents before we got married."

"Maybe you could talk them into coming here. They can afford the trip better than we can."

"My dad's too busy for that. What if they paid our way to Hawaii?"

"That would work but I still think timing is an issue. You better get going or time will be an issue for you. Don't worry. We'll talk about it later. Don't forget I've got a yard sale to do this weekend. We need to make that happen so that we can clean up your apartment and get your deposit back."

Chapter 119

I drove Susie to work and then purchased a copy of Sunday's paper. I found the want ads segment and went out onto the patio to smoke a cigarette while I looked them over. It had been seven months since I looked for a job and things were worst than before. Something was wrong. There were very few jobs listed. I went to the temp services I was familiar with but they had nothing to offer and the ESC was so packed I didn't even go in. My only guess was that the economy had changed while I was in rehab.

I needed to know what was happening but lunch time rolled around and as promised I took Susie a good lunch. We talked while she ate and I sat there enjoying her beauty. From the twinkle in her eyes, to the dimples in her cheeks, to the smile that crossed her beautiful face every time she realized she held me in her trace.

By 2 PM I wanted a buzz so I returned to the apartment, sat down at the kitchen table and smoked junk for a good hour. I sat there thinking about the bi-polar swings I was making between Susie and heroin. I was caught between the schizophrenic tendencies of an addict stuck between the desire to live sober and the harsh reality of sober living. Having seventeen packs of smack wasn't helping. Smoking it was not providing any relief. Instead of getting high, I got guilty. It felt like I was cheating on Susie.

Most days it was hard to tell who was on top. Sometimes it was Susie and sometimes it was the golden eye. When I threw away the rigs Susie won. When I spent hours smoking heroin the golden eye won. Heroin was giving me a run for my money. But that was wrong. I wouldn't allow there to be a running duel between Susie and junk. I knew what I stood to lose. We had now been together for ten months and were well on our way to celebrating our first year. We were having a child and getting married and that would slam the door on my past. Or would it? I could buck the tide with the best of them and there was a part of my brain that wanted smack no matter the consequences.

Chapter 120

Its funny how my mind works when left to its own devices. I had to change my focus or I was going to ruin the day. I had stop focusing on heroin. I had been in my head way too long so I turned my attention to the apartment. I put the paper away, washed several loads of clothes and decided on spaghetti for dinner. I knew that when she got off work she would be tired and hungry. I also knew that keeping her in plain view was the only chance I had of beating the golden eye.

Still I could not bring myself to throw away what remained of the heroin. Getting rid of it would have made my life so much easier. It would have killed off the addict in me, but I wasn't ready for that. Not yet. At five I went to pick up Susie and when she got in the truck I could tell that her day had been terrible. Hormones were giving her a run for her money and she cried all the way home. But I got her into the apartment, took her pocketbook and jacket and held her in my arms for a couple of minutes. I guided her to the bedroom, helped her out of her work clothes and into my Moody Blues t-shirt.

I helped her to the kitchen and sat her down in front of a plate of spaghetti, a spinach salad, garlic bread and ice tea. For the next forty-five minutes we ate and talked. We both had frustrating Mondays. There were no jobs in the paper and her boss was not going to give her anymore time off until it came time to have the baby. This seemed to be her biggest issue and she had sat there crying until I took her hand and said; "Everything will be okay. I'm going to take care of you and I'm looking for a job. Something will turn up. In the meantime just take care of yourself. Remember, work is only nine hours a day. The rest of the time you're here with me."

"I know. I don't know why I'm crying. I guess its hormones. I have taken a lot of time off but I had to. I guess I'm just tired. I need to take a nap after lunch but I can't because the phone won't stop ringing."

"Susie, your pregnant. We'll talk to the doctor and I'm sure he'll help you somehow. You've got to eat good food and get plenty of rest. From now on all you have to do is your job. I'll do everything else. I'll cook and clean. I'll do the shopping. I'll take care of the yard sale and clean up your old apartment. I'll take you back and forth to work and I'll keep you in good food."

"Thank you. It's no wonder I love you. When you break it down like that it takes the pressure off me."

"I've always told you that I would take care of you. Just keep your job so that you have insurance and we can eat and keep this apartment. Everything else will work itself out. We're going to be alright."

Chapter 121

While Susie moved to the couch I cleaned up the table, washed the dishes, put away the leftovers, then joined her on the couch. I took her feet in my hands and gently rubbed them until she was smiling. She held out her arms to me and said; "lay down with me." So I stretched out behind her and kissed her neck. In return Susie rolled onto her back and kissed me back, slow and gentle with every connection saying; "I love you." She guided my hand to her stomach and said; "put me to sleep."

"Let's just go to bed. It don't matter that its early. You need the rest."

We got up and I made sure the front door was locked while Susie brushed her teeth and headed for the bed. We crawled in and met in the middle where Susie again requested that I rub her stomach. I ran my fingers over her stomach, circling her belly button and gently rubbing our baby. She had went to sleep immediately and even though it was only seven-thirty, Susie had slept all night. I held her in my arms and watched the clock. At 6 AM I got up and fixed breakfast: Oatmeal, bananas, apples and oranges, sausage links, pancakes and syrup and all the milk she could drink.

As I was loading the table Susie came into the kitchen trying to wake up. She yawned and stretched and sat down. She watched as I fixed her a large bowl of oatmeal with fruit along with a side of sausages, pancakes with fruit and syrup and of course milk.

"I know you slept good, I didn't sleep a wink and you didn't wake up once. How do you feel?"

"Not bad. I slept good. I know we went to bed early and I'm glad we did because I do feel better."

"Good, Here's what I'm thinking. I'm going to start packing you snacks for your morning and after-noon breaks. Stuff like granola bars, trail mix, bananas, apples and water. I'll continue bringing you a good lunch and this should make you feel better all day."

Susie was eating, crying and smiling at the same time. When I saw that I grinned and took her hand. "I promised you I'd take care of you so as your needs grow I'll find ways to make your life and pregnancy easy. I'll take care of you everyday and at the end of the day you can sleep, safe and sound, in our bed."

Susie smiled through her tears and said; "I'm really very happy. You're always thinking of ways to take care of me and I love that. You pamper me and I love that. You're spoiling me rotten."

"That's what you get for falling in love with me. As the baby grows we'll find ways to keep up with healthy food and lots of rest. You worry about your job and the baby. I'll take care of everything else."

Susie finished her breakfast and took a shower while I cleaned up the kitchen. It took her about thirty minutes to get ready during which I made the bed and packed her snack bag. When she was ready we got in my truck and I drove her to work. We kissed before she got out of the truck and I reminded her that I would be back at twelve o'clock with lunch.

Chapter 122

I decided to make this a very special day for Susie. She needed a serious pick-me-up. So after taking her to work I went to the bank and withdrew three-thousand dollars. This emptied my savings account so now I had no money in the bank and only a few weeks of unemployment left to draw. The lack of spendable funds would stop my heroin use in its tracks and that was as good a way to quit as any.

I went to a local jewelry store and worked out a deal to buy a four-thousand dollar engagement ring for twenty-five hundred. It was huge, beautiful, exquisitely cut with a gold band and an eight point setting. The store put it in a hinged velvet box and with this taken care of I turned my focus to Susie's lunch.

I arrived at her job a few minutes early and waited her to come out the door. Once in the truck I drove to the park and helped her to our favorite picnic table. She sat there looking puzzled as I spread a table cloth before her, with linen napkins, her best china with silverware and wine glasses. Susie watched as I spread her lunch. Protein shakes, peanut butter jelly sandwiches, Doritos, chocolate cake, pickles, bottled water, sparkling apple cider, and "a surprise."

"What kind of surprise?" Susie asked, looking at me curiously. I told her not to worry and she smiled as she ran her fingertip around the edge of a plate; "I feel like the bloody queen. I never know what you're going to do next. You surprise me with something everyday but this is over the top so you must have something special up your sleeve or you wouldn't be teasing me."

"That's true. This is different. And I'm not teasing you.

267

You said the extra food made Monday go better so I'm kicking it up a notch. It could be that Mondays are always hell. You get just enough time off to remind you how much you hate work and then, before you know it, you're right back at it. I wish we were rich. Then we wouldn't have to worry about this shit."

Susie nodded her head, focused on eating and downed two shakes, a couple of sandwiches, half a bag of Doritos, several pickles, a piece of chocolate cake and two bottles of water. She ate like she was starved but that meant she was healthy and it's what I wanted to see. When she had finished I packed two sandwiches, the rest of the Doritos, two bananas and several bottles of water in a bag for her to take back to work. I cleaned up the table, popped the top on our sparkling cider and after filling our glasses I moved around the table and straddled the bench so that we could be close.

She watched me close in with the faintest of smiles and in her most innocent, child like voice said; "I spy with my little eye." I grinned at her and said; "I know we've talked about doing this together but I wanted today to be a very special day for you so I did it on my own." I pulled the ring box from my pocket and opened it before her. She gasped, took the box from me and sat there for a good minute just looking at the ring.

"Oh my god...it's beautiful. Wow. Look at you. You are something else. You know that? You really are. One surprise after another. This is insane. Completely over the top."

I removed the ring from its box, took her hand and slid it onto her finger. "I know I've asked you this before, but I'm asking you again: Will you marry me?" She looked at me with tears running down her face. She turned on the bench, wrapped her legs around my waist and pulled herself to me. She seemed lost in the joy of what it symbolized and had thrown her arms around my neck and after an enthusiastic kiss had said; "Oh yes, I will marry you. Oh my god... You've made me the happiest girl in the world. You really topped yourself this time. I am always amazed by the ways you make love to me."

We wrapped our arms and legs around each other and sat there on that park bench starring deeply into each others eyes. "I love you Susie, you deserve the best of everything. But it's time for you to go back to work so take this food and eat it this afternoon. Keep your energy levels high. That will make for a better day." She whispered "I love you" and kissed me soft and slow.

"Okay, I'm ready. Thanks for the loving, you've really made my day."

I handed her my afternoon care package and we drove back to her office. As she got out of the truck I reminded her that I would be back a five-thirty to pick her up. "That's only four hours from now, so pace yourself. Don't let anything upset you. Just enjoy the day. It's only work."

"Don't worry about that. This ring is going to blow everybody's mind. It may even help me with my boss. At least he'll see that I'm serious about getting married and starting a family. I love you."

"I love you too. Be good to yourself. I'll be back to get you at five-thirty."

Chapter 123

It had been a busy morning and I was ready for a break. So I headed back to the apartment and spent an hour smoking junk. I got a good buzz going and drove over to Susie's apartment where I spent the next few hours boxing up yard sale items. When I ran out of boxes I visited a few grocery stores and once I had enough I returned to the apartment and continued boxing priced items. There were things that still needed pricing and I put them off to one side. Before leaving I smoked a couple of bowls and that got me thinking about what I would fix Susie for dinner.

Chinese food came to mind. It was an easy fix so at five o'clock I called in an order, picked Susie up and then stopped by for the food. My timing was perfect and by six we were back at the apartment opening our containers and filling our plates. Susie was bubbling with excitement. Everyone at work had been blown away by her engagement ring and the office had talked all afternoon about when she was going to get married.

Of course she didn't know because we hadn't set a date and when she asked if I had called my parents I had to say no. I had worked on the yard sale all afternoon so I could be finished by Friday. That would let me clean up her apartment Friday evening and have the yard sale on Saturday. She could get her deposit back and that would be the end of that.

Once we had finished eating Susie had watched me clean up and when I had finished she was standing there with her arms spread wanting a hug. We melted together, with our baby in the middle, and after a few minutes Susie had said; "This has been a wonderful day... let's go to bed... I feel like making love." I scooped her up and she had laughed as I carried her to bed and gently sat her on the edge. While she undressed I stepped out on the patio and smoked a cigarette as well as a bowl of heroin. I re-entered the bedroom, took off my clothes and slipped into bed. I worked my way to Susie and found her naked. All she wore was her new engagement ring and she was more than ready to make love.

She was accepting and passionate and we spent the next hour loving on each other. There was no need to hurry and she needed to be treated gently. It was a wonderful way to end an incredible day and our love once again achieved new heights. Susie reveled in our love. She loved the fact that our sex life was still as satisfying as it had been the first time we made love. Maybe more. She know how to ask for what she wanted and was very happy with the results.

For the second night in a row she had went to sleep with a smile on her face and she had slept all night without waking. On the other hand I spent another night holding her and thinking. Sleep eluded me and I knew this would eventually become a serious problem. In my decades old battle with insomnia I had only found a few things helped me get descent sleep. Valium, Xanax, vodka and heroin. Since finding my stash I had done a good job of taking care of Susie while keeping my smack consumption low. If insomnia set in, migraine headaches would follow, and for me migraine headaches were always three day events. Once the cycle of insomnia and migraines set in I would not be to take care of Susie.

I was being pulled into a bind of my own making and I had precious few solutions. I could not help but wonder what was going on with the job market. There didn't seem to be any jobs available and I made a mental note to get to the bottom of that tomorrow. I had to get a job before I got too hot. I still had my Methadone card so I made another mental note to start using it the next day. If I could stop using smack long enough to get a job I could then subtly smoke heroin and nobody would know the difference. This was the only way to handle my insomnia and it was the one thing Susie couldn't help me with.

Chapter 124

I finally went to sleep around 3AM and as a result I overslept. Susie's doctor appointment was at nine and we had both slept until seven-thirty. That made for a hurried morning but I had made up some of the lost time by going to McDonalds for biscuits and Cokes while Susie took a shower. I was not sure what she liked so I had bought a variety just to make sure I got something she would eat. As it turned out Susie was hungry and she had ate two biscuits while getting ready.

She was excited about the doctor's appointment because it was her first sonogram so we may be able to learn the babies sex. I was cool with that because if we knew its sex we could tell people what to buy Susie for her baby shower. I didn't know much about baby showers but I promised her that if she didn't get one I would take her out for dinner and buy her a lot of baby related presents. She laughed and said that I treated her better than her co-workers did anyway.

I loved telling her that I was her "baby daddy" and she had no problem with me owning my presence in her life. We were slowly becoming a family. While she got ready we talked about her boss, how many months she thought she was along and how much time she wanted off at the time of the baby's birth. I had a serious question I had wanted to ask more than any other so I just asked her straight up; "Do you think my heroin use could possibly mess up our baby? Maybe twisted up my chromosomes."

I didn't know enough about pregnancy to have too many questions but that one had always stuck in my throat and I had worried about this ever since learning she was pregnant with my child. Susie thought about it for a minute, and I watched the gears in her brain turn as she slowly did the math. It took her awhile but eventually she said; "I wouldn't worry about that. The baby's been in me for four months, maybe a little more, and by my count you were only hot for two weeks at the very beginning of our pregnancy. I was clean when we got pregnant, you overdosed the very next week and you've been clean ever since. Now we're doing everything we can to make sure me and the baby are healthy so I really don't think we have anything to worry about."

Chapter 125

The OB-GYN appointment had went as planned and while the doctor performed a sonogram he could not tell the babies sex. The picture simply wasn't clear enough. A haze of some sort enveloped the fetus and he had a hard time hearing the babies heartbeat. He was clearly rattled by this but he had recovered and said that it was early in the babies development and everything was just fine. But I was watching his face and could tell that he had seen this before and it was not good news. He didn't say anything that might upset Susie and had scheduled an appointment four weeks later.

He prescribed pre-natal vitamins and ended the visit by saying that while the fetus seemed a little small there was no point worrying. A lot of times the view he got depended on how the fetus was positioned. All in all we were in there for thirty minutes and I had Susie at work in fifteen minutes so she was only forty-five minutes late. From there I went to the grocery store and bought one-hundred and fifty dollars worth of groceries. I filled the kitchen with food of every kind. Good food, junk food, Susie's favorites, staples. I had bought at least two weeks worth and decided that today I would fix Susie vegetable soup, ham and cheese sandwiches, peanut butter crackers, chocolate chip cookies and Sprite.

For her afternoon snack I packed granola bars, cookies, an apple and several bottles of water. I had a refrigerator full of leftovers so I decided we would have spinach salads and Chinese food for dinner. If she was still hungry after all that I would feed her leftover spaghetti and garlic toast. I had about forty-five minutes before meeting her for lunch and I spent a good part of it smoking junk. I ended up with a subtle buzz, nothing overwhelming or noticeable, but it relaxed me and made my world a better place.

Susie wouldn't understand that and keeping those two worlds separate was paramount. All I had to do was keep her entertained and lunch was a great, mid-day way to do that. So I met her at twelve sharp and took her to the park, to our favorite picnic table. Lunch went great. She was happy. Her boss was treating her better and that took a lot of pressure off her. She wasn't crying anymore and that was a victory in my book.

I smiled as she worked her way through everything I had brought. I smiled. She was radiant and care-free. Pregnant, engaged and happy. There was no way I was going to screw that up. When we were finished I took her back to work and after a really nice, soft, slow kiss I said; "See you in a few hours. Be happy and don't forget to eat your snacks."

With that I headed into town to the ESC office. I waited in line for about forty-five minutes and when I got to a counselor I asked about new jobs that I could apply for. We looked at several different sectors but the job market had dried up. The economy was slow and the unemployment rate was up. I asked about an extension in my unemployment payments and after checking was told that I had a final sixteen weeks to draw. That was good enough for now and I was told to come back next week for an update.

Chapter 126

I drove away calculating. I had thirteen packets of heroin and no money in the bank. I was broke. I had spent it all on heroin and Susie's engagement ring. I had sixteen weeks of unemployment compensation coming and Susie's paycheck would pick up the slack. The possibility of a bad economy meant more people would lose their job and that would make finding any kind of job hard to do. I would have to tell Susie about this in a way she would understand. But for now I had a few hours to kill so I went back to the apartment and settled into an hour of smoking heroin. I went through half a pack, caught a pretty good buzz and then headed out to pick Susie up. My mind was pleasantly drugged and for a moment I let it soar with the clouds. But then she was there waving at me from the office door and I had pulled up to her so she didn't have to walk.

"Hello beautiful...how did your afternoon go?"

"Great. I think I'm finally back in my bosses good graces. He told me if there was anything I needed to let him know. I think he's softening up and that will certainly make my life easier."

"Just don't ask for anything until its absolutely necessary. If you don't miss work and wait long enough you might build up enough good-will to get the time you want off when the babies born."

The next few days were business as usual. Susie finished pricing the yard sale items while I cleaned her apartment from top to bottom. I got permission from my apartment manager to have the yard sale in the common area of the complex. I then spent two days hanging fliers on every apartment door in a three square mile area. On Friday I loaded my truck with yard sale items while Susie turned her keys in and did a walk through of her apartment. The manager had been pleased and cut her a check for three-hundred and fifty dollars. It represented progress and turning in her keys closed the door on her past.

When we got back to our apartment I helped her inside and while she got into her t-shirt I ordered a pizza from the local pizzeria and fixed her a large glass of ice tea. While we waited for the pizza man I reminded her that the next day was yard sale day. I didn't want her help. I didn't even want her up there. She agreed and after eating we curled up on the couch and it wasn't long before Susie was ready for bed. It's what I wanted and after securing the apartment I joined her.

That night the gray man appeared in my dreams and again, when he opened his mouth to speak, ashes and dirt spilled forth covering his chest. He seemed desperate to tell me something and grew more and more agitated when I couldn't understand what he was trying to say. He slung his head from side to side until blood flew from his eyes and mingled with the ashes that poured from his mouth, ran down his face to pool on the floor at his feet. When he was finally exhausted by his attempt to communicate he fell into a pile of ashes beside the bed. The gray man was a harbinger of bad news, however I couldn't understand what he was trying to say.

At 4 AM I got up, fixed a pot of coffee and set up the yard sale in the apartment common area. By 6 AM I had my first customers. People came from everywhere and at times it was all I could do to keep up with everyone. By lunch I had collected almost three-hundred dollars and by three-thirty I was up to four-hundred and fifty dollars. It had been a whopping success and there was so little left that I had put it all in one box, wrote "free" on it, and put it in the laundry room. The day had been exhausting but I had done a good job and was proud to hand Susie four-hundred and fifty dollars.

The yard sale I had been a whopping success. She tried to smile but I could tell something was wrong and when I asked her about it she had said she didn't feel good. She had ate throughout the day and slept on and off. She should be feeling fine and she couldn't explain it other than to say she just didn't feel good. As the week progressed Susie began having terrible bouts of morning sickness and horrible stomach cramps. We worked very hard to get over this hump but the morning sickness got worse and the stomach cramps doubled her over in pain.

We called her OB-GYN and he scheduled her for first thing in the morning. That night Susie's pain intensified and around 3 AM she had started hemorrhaging massive amounts of blood. Her stomach cramps were so bad they left her sobbing in pain and I had to carry her to the truck. Once at the hospital I carried her into the emergency room and she was immediately taken into an operating room. For the next three hours doctors tried to stabilize her but they were helpless to stop what was happening and at 6 AM she miscarried. She had lost a lot of blood and had to be given several replacement pints.

Because of the savage nature of her miscarriage, she had been heavily sedated and checked into ICU. She slept for three days and on the fourth day she was weaned from the drugs and slowly returned to consciousness. She was moved to a private room and the doctors who had worked on her stopped by to explain that the fetus had died "In Utero." This meant that her body had tried to birth the baby before it was ready. It meant that there was something fatally wrong with the fetus.

This explained why the sonogram had been hazy and why her OB-GYN had not been able to hear the babies heartbeat. There was no explanation for what had happened or why it happened which meant there was no simple answer. Sometimes miscarriages just happen. It didn't mean we couldn't try again. Many couples who had miscarriages went on to give birth to healthy children.

Chapter 127

But for Susie nothing would ever be the same. The magic that bound us as one now lay broken and she fled into a dark, loveless world from which she refused to return. Nothing I said or tried to do made any difference. She didn't want me around. She didn't want me touching her, or talking to her, or being in the same room with her. When she did talk it was to blame my heroin use for the loss of her baby and the doctors had said that it was a remote possibility. If the doctors hadn't said that I may have stood a chance. I might have won Susie back. But their "remote possibility" destroyed the connection we had and there was no repairing the damage.

I tried getting through to her by telling her that while this was a sad outcome we could get over it. We were young. We had time. We could get past this. But she didn't hear me. I made no impression and its painful to admit but I guess right then I knew we were over. We would never be the same, would never love each other the same. So I sat by the door hoping she would snap out of it. But she didn't and when she was released I took her back to the apartment. She said nothing and had stayed just long enough to pack a suitcase of clothes. As far as she was concerned where she went was none of my business.

Before leaving she slipped her engagement ring off and laid it on the kitchen table. She left without saying a word but her actions spoke volumes. The golden eye whispered in my brain; "Bet you wished you had those rigs now. What's ya' gonna do? It's just another heartbreak and it's all about the pain. This time I'm gonna take you down so low you'll never come back. You won't even try."

The golden eye wanted me to finish what I had started before meeting Susie. I turned to it to ease my pain and spent the next several days smoking heroin nonstop. My lungs ached from the smoke. Susie made it pretty clear that she wasn't coming back so a knock at the front door startled me. I opened it half expecting to see her but instead it was a couple girls from her office who handed me a note that read:

"Steve – Let them pack my clothes. I have sold the furniture to a used furniture store. They will pick it up tomorrow. They won't buy the mattress or box spring so you can have them. I'm moving back to Hawaii. Don't contact me. I have nothing to say to you. Susie."

I sat on the patio while they packed her clothes. They left Susie's house key on the kitchen table. While sitting there I remembered my "gray man" dream and realized that Susie's miscarriage was what he had been foretelling. Blood and death, graves and dirt – vampires and junkies. They went hand in hand and now the dream made perfect sense. When I realized this, all the life in my body seemed to flow away and once again I dwelt among the walking dead. I had been through this before. Shattered love was the story of my life. Where was I supposed to go now? My response to the pain was predictable.

Chapter 128

The only thing that saved my life was a call from my mother informing me that my father's health was rapidly declining and she needed me to come home and help her take care of him. I said okay. I took Susie's ring back to the jewelry store and asked for a refund. The clerk had took one look at me and after a brief conversation with his store manager he had counted out my refund in one-hundred bills. As if he had seen this before he looked at me and said; "Sorry man. Better luck next time."

There wouldn't be a "next time" for me. Not in this life time. If I hadn't promised my Mom to help her care for my father I would have spent the next several days perfecting the hit that would kill me. But I had promised and that meant closing up shop in Winston Salem and moving back to Yadkinville. I didn't like this idea because living in the country presented a different set of challenges. I spent the rest of the week smoking heroin and packing my clothes. My mind slowly rolled over and once again it became my worse enemy.

Once again heroin became my armor and my weapon of self destruction. I wanted to soar into the heavens of junk and I didn't care if I ever came back. This was a state of mind I was all too familiar with. I took the twenty-five hundred I had gotten from the jewelry store and spent it all on heroin. I set some aside for immediate use and packed the rest in the boxes that held my clothing. I also purchased several cases of vodka and a couple ten packs of rigs. My death was back on schedule.

I had just finished packing my clothes when the used furniture company showed up. They cleaned out the apartment in less than fifteen minutes leaving me with nothing but the mattress and box spring, a few decorations and the utensils in the kitchen. They had bought it all without looking at it so I doubt they paid her more than a few hundred dollars. She didn't need the money. She was suffering and she was making sure I suffered to. With few exceptions the apartment looked exactly like it did the first night I had brought her home. That was all I needed to start shooting heroin again and I spent the next few weeks making sure my technique was flawless.

Chapter 129

But mom called again and this time I cleaned the apartment one last time, emptied out the refrigerator, cut off the utilities and turned my keys over to management. After a good-bye walk through they had refunded my deposit, in cash. I headed underground. I needed very little human contact and had drove to Yadkin County as if headed to a funeral. For the next two years I helped my mother take care of my father. The older he got the more restless he became. To calm him down I would ride him around in my truck. We would aimlessly ride for hours and over the months we hit every road in Yadkin County.

He made it to ninety-four and fought death right up to the end. But the end did come and that left me and mom with the farm. Initially it came with it an extensive workload. There were acres of grass to keep mowed, dilapidated barns to tear down, overgrown trees to be cut down, house repairs to be made. It was to much for me to handle alone so I leased everything but the house and surrounding yard to a local farmer for one-hundred dollars an acre, cash money, paid to me at the end of every season.

I guess the first time I realized I had lived my original nightmare right up to the final "puff" was the day I made peace with my past and turned my attention to the only choice I had left. From that moment forward my sole purpose was to just live. Deep side of me there has always been a strong desire to die doing battle with a strong desire to live and the strong desire to die was usually winning.

But my life is now nothing like it once was. I've got a dog, a truck and a garden. I'm drawing Social Security Disability so I've got enough money to keep things going. I have no real complaints. I think about Susie a lot. Probably more than anyone would deem healthy but I can't stop the flood. Sadness always drowns any happiness I feel and vodka drowns the sadness. As ironic as it may seem, missing Susie's not the hardest part. The hardest part is knowing that I once knew her, once held her in my arms and was once loved by her.

Those are the facts that break my heart. Over the years Xanax and vodka has turned me into a ghost. I'm the shadow of a person I barely remember. No friends, no family. I don't go anywhere unless its absolutely necessary. No one visits and that's alright. My parents are dead, all my friends are dead and most people look right straight through me.

I spend a lot of time thinking about the women in my past and it always leaves me with more questions than answers. Could Melinda have been going to see a doctor on the morning she was killed because she thought she was pregnant? Was Diane pregnant when she was murdered? Losing these wonderful women and imagining the possibility that they were pregnant with my child when they died is horrible. I can't answer these questions. They torture me a lot. Was I really to blame for Susie's miscarriage?

Could the blood and ashes of the gray man dream represent this horrible event and could the syringe he used to drain me of blood represent my own death? Then again maybe the miscarriage was the third death. Maybe when he bled me dry it was a sign of my life to come. Alone and dying, here on the farm.

Chapter 130

In 2012, I turned fifty-two. I'm still alive and that is, without question, a miracle. Maybe a little luck, maybe its fate, maybe its destiny. Maybe pain is progress. Maybe it makes you stronger and as a result you last longer. You get tough. It turns you into a soldier hardened by your personal war and years of endless marching. You learn to weather the storm, even if it means lashing yourself to the mast. I never got out in front of my addiction and by the time I learned to stand on my own, I found myself standing alone. As Mick Jagger so properly put it; "It's not easy facing up when your whole world is black."

It's been eighteen years since I moved back to Yadkinville. Eighteen years since I last saw Susie. But I think about her a lot and remember her like it was yesterday. I hope she found the love she deserves. I hope one day she'll find it in her heart to forgive me.

As for me. I've been tested beyond my ability to endure. But I'm still here. I've learned to take life one day at a time. To relax. To be still. To sit in a rocking chair and just rock. Of course I no longer use heroin but it is an undeniable part of my life. I'm truly amazed to have lived long enough to tell you this story. Don't think of my life as a cautionary tale. You're not going to learn a lot studying my example.

Some broken hearts mend while others are too shattered to ever love again. The pain can be unreal and there's no guarantee you'll recover. I've long outlived my life. All that's left is death. So I take it one day at a time and I don't take on more than I can bear. One day my broken heart will simply fall apart. One day sadness will overwhelm any desire I have to live and I will pass away. For now I'm satisfied to live my life somewhere between desire and despair. The end will come soon enough.

Printed in Great Britain
by Amazon